alberta anglican politicians
1883-1999

other works by austin mardon

Alberta Catholic Politicians
What's in a Name?
Designed by Providence
Seven Days in Moscow
Who's Who in Federal Politics in Alberta
The Liberals in Power
When Kitty met the Ghost

alberta anglican politicians 1883-1999

austin a. mardon & ernest g. mardon

edited by carmen wu

golden meteorite press
edmonton alberta canada

© 2013 copyright by Golden Meteorite Press.

All rights reserved. No part of this publication may be reproduced, stored in a retrieval system or transmitted, in any form or by any means, without prior written consent of the publisher or a licence from The Canadian Copyright Licensing Agency (Access Copyright). For an Access Copyright licence, visit www.accesscopyright.ca or call: 1-(800)-893- 5777.

Cover design and typeset by Bianca Ho
Edited by Carmen Wu

Published by Golden Meteorite Press.

126 Kingsway Garden
Post Office Box 34181
Edmonton, Alberta, Canada T5G 3G4
Telephone: 1-(780)-378-0063
Email: aamardon@yahoo.ca
Website: www.austinmardon.org

Library and Archives Canada Cataloguing in Publication
Mardon, Austin A. (Austin Albert), author
Alberta Anglican politicians, 1883-1999 / Austin A. Mardon & Ernest G. Mardon ; edited by Carmen Wu.
ISBN 978-1-897472-87-3 (pbk.)
1. Politicians--Alberta--Biography. 2. Anglicans--Alberta--Biography. 3. Alberta--Politics and government. I. Mardon, Ernest G., 1928-, author II. Wu, Carmen, editor III. Title.
FC3655.M363 2013   971.23009'9   C2013-903513-3

dedicated to bishop john privett

biographies

entries

alphabetically ordered

a. 10 / b. 16 / c. 35

d. 52 / e. 62 / f. 65

g. 69 / h. 75 / i. 89

j. 92 / k. 98 / l. 102

m. 111 / n. 120 / o. 123

p. 126 / q. 134 / r. 136

s. 145 / t. 162 / w. 165

a

james allen 'boomer' adair

Born May 13, 1929 at Edmonton, son of James W. Adair and his wife Beatrice Shewfelt. He was of English descent and an Anglican. Educated at Mayerthorpe and Athabasca, he became a Peace River radio sportscaster. Later he served on the executive of CKYL radio station. In 1960 he married Joyce Helena Johnson, daughter of the Reverend C. Alvin Johnson of Wetaskiwin.

J. Allen Adair returned as the Progressive Conservative member for Peace River in 1971. He was re-elected five times and sat in the Legislature for 23 years. During the period he served as the Minister Responsible for Northern Development (1974), Minister of Recreation, Parks and Wildlife (1975), Minister of Tourism and Small Business (1979), and Minister of Transportation and Telecommunications (1986). In 1993 he did not seek re-election, and retired from politics at the age of 64. He died in 1998.

[See: Canadian Who's Who, 1981]

12 frank pierpoint appleby

Born December 23, 1922 at Stocks, Alberta, son of Ernest W. Appleby and Fanny Mary Tench. He was of English descent and an Anglican. He was educated at Smoky Lake. During World War II he enlisted in the Royal Canadian Air Force and saw active service as a sergeant in France. In the January 1945 special 'Province-at-large' Armed Forces (Air) election, he was an unsuccessful candidate. He states that he attended Alberta College, Edmonton; University of British Columbia; University of Saskatchewan; University of Toronto; Mount Allison University, Nova Scotia; University of Alberta and Oxford University, England. He became a school teacher in Athabasca.

Frank Appleby returned as the Progressive Conservative member for Athabasca in 1971. He sat in the Legislature as a government backbencher for 11 years. In 1982, he did not seek re-election, retiring from politics at the age of 61.

[See: Canadian Parliamentary Guide, 1980]

frederick william archer

Born August 7, 1859 in Ireland, son of Charles P. Archer and Anna Mills. He was an Anglican of Anglo-Irish descent. His ancestors had lived on the land in County Wicklow granted to them by the Crown since the 16th century. Educated in Wicklow and Dublin, he came to Canada in 1883, settling in Innisfail where he became a lumber merchant and farmer. He served under Col. Boulton in Boulton's Mounted Cavalry during the Northwest Rebellion of 1885.

Frederick W. Archer returned as the Conservative member for Innisfail in 1913. He sat in the Legislature as an opposition member for one term. In 1917 he was defeated by Liberal Daniel J. Morkeberg and retired from politics at the age of 58. He died in 1936 at Innisfail.

[See: Canadian Parliamentary Guide, 1917]

14 herbert joseph ash

Born March 13, 1878 at London, England, son of Joseph Robert Ash and Eleanor Cole Rhodes. He was of English descent and an Anglican. He was educated at Borough Polytechnic. He emigrated to Canada as a young man and became a well-known famer in the Ghost Pine Creek area near Red Deer. He served as a municipal district councilor, reeve and school trustee.

H. J. Ash returned as the Social Credit member for Olds in 1935 after being hand-picked by William Aberhart as the party's candidate. He sat in the Legislature as a government backbencher for five years. He was among the 'insurgent' who tried to topple the government in 1937. In 1940 he ran as an Independent Social Creditor, but was defeated by Norman Cook, the official Social Credit candidate. He then retired from politics at the age of 62.

[See: Canadian Parliamentary Guide, 1940]

patrick harvey ashby

Born October 17, 1890 in Sussex, England, son of Frederick Ashby and his wife, Fanny Ashby. He was of English descent and an Anglican. He attended Wadham College at Oxford University. When he came to Canada he settled in Edmonton and attended the University of Alberta. He became an Edmonton district farmer.

Patrick Harvey Ashby returned as the Social Credit member for the Edmonton East riding in 1945. He sat in the House of Commons for four years as an opposite member. In 1949 he was an unsuccessful independent candidate and then retired from politics at the age of 60.

[See: Canadian Who's Who, 1958]

b

gerald william 'ged' baldwin, q.c.

Born January 18. 1907 at Palmerston, New Zealand, son of Vaudrey Balwin, a lawyer, and his wife, the former Miss Richardson. He was an Anglican. As a young man, his father had travelled to the Klondike gold fields in 1989. He came to Canada as a child and was educated in Edmonton, graduating from the University of Alberta in Arts and then in Law. After being admitted to the Alberta Bar, he joined his father's Peace River legal firm. He was an unsuccessful provincial candidate in 1935. During World War II he enlisted in the Canadian Army and saw active service as an artillery officer in the Northwest Europe campaign of 1944-45. In 1957 he was an unsuccessful federal candidate.

Ged Baldwin returned as the Progressive Conservative member for the Peace River riding in 1958. He sat in the House of Commons for 22 years. He was referred to as "the conscience of the House of Commons". In 1980, he did not seek re-election and retired from politics at the age of 73.

[See: Canadian Who's Who, 1980]

h. raymond ballard

Born February 5, 1918 at Provost, Alberta, son of William Thomas Ballard and his wife Marie Armstrong. He was of English descent and an Anglican. He was educated at Lloydminster and attended the University of British Columbia. He became a Calgary businessman and a chartered accountant. He served as a city alderman from 1962 to 1966.

H. Ray Ballard returned as the Progressive Conservative member for the Calgary South riding in 1965 and sat in the House of Commons for three years. In 1968 he was defeated by Liberal lawyer Patrick M. Mahoney. His daughter, Patricia Leigh Black attended the University of Calgary, graduating in Commerce and becoming a business consultant. Ms. Black returned as the Progressive Conservative member for Calgary Foothills in 1989. She was re-elected in 1993 and again in 1997. In December 1992 Premier Klein appointed her to the cabinet as Minister of Energy.

[See: Canadian Parliamentary Guide, 1979 and 1997]

george russell barker

Born October 26, 1881 at Melbourne, Australia, son of Col. John Barker and Christina Leslie. He was of Scottish descent and an Anglican. His father was military officer in charge of the Melbourne Royal Mint. Young Barker's grandfather was the proprietor of a large sheep ranch in the State of Victoria, Australia. He returned to England to attend Bradfield College, Berkshire and later served as a British and Indian army officer in the artillery. After leaving the army in 1904, he came to Canada and became a landowner in the Lac Ste. Anne region. He was an unsuccessful candidate in the 1914 general election.

Russell Barker returned as the Conservative member for Lac Ste. Anne in 1917. He sat in the Legislature for four years as a member of the opposition. It was said at the time when he was a member that he lived in the largest house between Edmonton and Dawson City, Yukon. In 1921, he did not seek re-election and retired from politics.

[See: Canadian Parliamentary Guide, 1921]

arthur beaumont, k.c.

Born December 19, 1891 at Ballinrobe, county Mayo, Ireland, son of William Beaumont and his wife Helen Mayne. He was of Anglo-Irish descent and an Anglican. He attended Budlin's St. Andrew's College and was admitted to the Irish Bar in 1913. He came to Canada in the following year as an officer with the Canadian Mounted Rifles in the Canadian Expeditionary Force. He saw active service on the Western Front. After the war he practiced law in Killam and later in Ponoka.

Arthur Beaumont was an unsuccessful provincial candidate for the Conservative party in the 1926 election. He ran against former premier John E. Brownlee. From 1936 to 1948 he served as a police magistrate in Lethbridge. In 1958 Justice Minister Davie Fulton appointed Arthur Beaumont as a judge of the Southern Alberta District Court. In 1923 he had married Ida Mae Devine of Quebec City. Their son, Henry Beaumont, Q.C. is a Calgary lawyer. Arthur Beaumont was a member of the Dominion Synod of the Anglican Church for more than two decades. He died March 19, 1964 while still on the Bench at the age of 73.

george ernest bell

Born November 21, 1883 at Malton, Ontario. He was of Anglo-Irish descent and an Anglican. Educated at Brampton, he attended the Toronto Normal School, qualifying as a teacher. He taught school for ten years. Keen on sports, he was a member of the champion All Saints football team. In 1910 he moved to Alberta, settling at Shamrock, near Gleichem, when he became a prominent farmer. On the outbreak of WWI, he enlisted in the Canadian Army. He went overseas with the Canadian Expeditionary Force and saw active service on the Western Front where he was seriously wounded.

George E. Bell returned as the Social Credit member for Gleichen in 1944. He sat in the Legislature for 18 years. In 1963 he did not seek re-election and retired at the age of 80. He died in 1967 at Strathmore.

[See: Canadian Parliamentary Guide, 1963]

frederick johnstone 'jack' bigg

Born May 26, 1912 at Meskanaw, Saskatchewan, son of Frederick J. Bigg, Senior and his wife Ethel Traill. He was of Scottish descent and an Anglican. Educated at Prince Albert Collegiate Institute, he attended the University of Saskatchewan, graduating in Arts, and then the University of Toronto, graduating in Law. As a young man he enlisted in the R.C.M.P. and served in the force until 1940. During the war he enlisted in the Canadian army and saw active service in Europe. After the war he rejoined the R.C.M.P. While in the force he attended the University of Toronto. Upon retiring from the force he was admitted to the Alberta Bar and practiced law in Westlock.

In 1967, F.J. 'Jack' Bigg returned as the Progressive Conservative member for Athabasca. He sat in the House of Commons for fifteen years. In 1972, he did not seek re-election, retired from politics and returned to his law practice. He died a short time later. In 1958, it had been said that it was a frosty Friday when Indians, Metis, trappers, and hunter of Northeast Alberta voted for an ex-policeman. The riding had for eighteen years been a Liberal stronghold.

[See: Canadian Who's Who, 1967]

william john blair

Born October 13, 1875 at Embro, Ontario, son of John Blair and his wife Ellen Smyth. He was of Anglo-Irish descent and an Anglican. Educated at Woodstock, he attended the Toronto School of Practical Science, graduating as a mining engineer. He came to Alberta in 1906 and homesteaded in the Provost district becoming a prominent farmer in the area. He was an unsuccessful provincial candidate in the 1913 election.

William J. Blair returned as the Unionist Pro-government member of the Battle River riding in 1917. He sat in the House of Commons for four years. In 1921 he did not seek re-election and retired from federal politics. Later he served as the Alberta Conservative leader. He was succeeded in this position by A.A. McGillivray in August 1925.

[See: Canadian Parliamentary Guide, 1918]

robert john bogle

Born August 29, 1943 at Calgary, son of Robert Bogle and his wife Phoebe Alberta Orford. He was of English descent and an Anglican. Educated at Warner and Milk River, he attended Calgary's Mount Royal College, the University of Lethbridge and Montreal's Sir George Williams University. He became a school teacher in Milk River and served on the Milk River town council from 1969 to 1975. In 1977 he married Dr. Elizabeth C. Lewke of Calgary. In the same year he was an unsuccessful candidate in the provincial election.

Robert John Bogle returned as the Progressive Conservative member for Taber-Warner in 1975; he sat in the Legislature for 18 years. He served as the minister responsible for native Affairs in 1975, Minister of Social Services and Community Health in 1979, and Minister Utilities and Telecommunications from 1982 to 1986. In 1993, he did not seek re-election and retired from politics.

[See: Canadian Parliamentary Guide, 1993]

arthur moran boutillier

Born October 16, 1869 at Halifax, Nova Scotia, son of Esrom Boutillier and his wife Anne Spear. He was of French and Anglo-Irish descent and an Anglican. He was educated at the Halifax Academy and came to Alberta as a young man. In 1904 he became a homesteader in the Eagle district and later was active in the United Farmers of Alberta movement and in civic politics, serving as Treasurer of the Municipal District of Eagle during carious terms from 1904 to 1924.

A.M. Boutillier returned as the UFA member for the Vegreville riding in 1925 and sat in the House of Commons for less than a year. He did not seek re-election in the 1926 general election. In the 1940 federal election he was an unsuccessful CCF candidate for Vegreville.

richard henry, viscount **boyle** [6th earl of shannon]

Born May 15, 1860 at Castle Maryn, County of Cork, Ireland, son of Henry Bentinck, 5th Earl of Shannon and his first wife Lady Blanche Emma Lascelles, daughter of the Earl of Harwood. One of his ancestors had served as the Speaker of the Irish House of Commons in the 18th century. He was of Anglo-Irish descent and an Anglican. The Earls of Shannon were a branch of the house of Boyle, the Earls of Cork. As a young man he served as a lieutenant in the King's Own Rifle Corps.

Coming to Canada, he served as a sergeant in the Northwest Mounted Police at Fort George. After his discharge he became a rancher. During the 1885 Northwest Rebellion he commanded a militia unit and saw active service. Richard Henry Boyle returned as the member for Macleod on the N.W.T. Executive Council. In 1895 he married Mellie Thompson and on the death of his father in 1896 he returned to the United Kingdom and assumed the title. His lordship died December 11, 1906 at the age of 46.

[See: Burke's Peerage and Baronage, 1970]

frederick deryl bradley

Born September 17, 1949 at Blairmore, son of James Clark Bradley and his wife Thelma E. Pinkney. He was of Anglican descent and an Anglican. Educated at Blairmore, he attended the University of Alberta and became a merchant in Blairmore.

Fred D. Bradley returned as the Progressive Conservative Member for Pincher Creek-Crownsnest in 1975 and sat in the Legislature for 18 years. He served as the Minister of Environment from 1982 to 1986. In 1993 he did not seek re-election and retired from politics at the age of 43.

[See: Canadian Parliamentary Guide, 1993]

alwyn bramley-moore

Born in 1878 at London, England, son of the Rev. W. Bramley-Moore and his wife. He was of ethnic English descent and an Anglican. He came to Ontario in 1895 and in 1904 to Alberta as a Bar Colonist and homesteaded near Lloydminster.

Alwyn Bramley-Moore returned as the Liberal member for Alexandra (Lloydminster) in 1909. He sat in the Legislature as a vocal government back bencher. In 1913 he did not seek re-election and retired from politics. He became well-known after the publication of Canada and Her Colonies or Home Rule for Alberta in 1911. The book dealt extensively with such longstanding issues with the relationship between the provinces and the federal government and the ownership of natural resources. He took up the cause of Alberta against what he defined as "Eastern tyranny" and defined what he saw as "conflicting interests of the East and the West". One of his statements could be said to reflect the philosophy of many of the Canadian provinces today: "The true principle that must be embodied in any constitution undertaking to hold together an aggregate of the national units, by they racial or geographical, the true principle is the fullest autonomy for the separate units." Indeed, Bramley-Moore went so far as to advocate eventual secession, but only as a mechanism to enhance Alberta's bargaining position vis-à-vis the federal government. A thought worthy of any contemporary Alberta patriot! Alwyn Bramley-Moore died as a result of injuries sustained while on active service at Vimy Ridge in April, 1916.

[See: Canadian Parliamentary Guide, 1913; Edmonton Journal, June 4/5/6, 1980 quoting Canada and Her Colonies]

w. fletcher bredin

Born in 1857 at Glengarry, Ontario, son of a farmer. He was of Anglo-Irish descent and an Anglican. He came to Manitoba as a young man in 1877 to farm near Winnipeg. Later he travelled widely across North America. While on a trip down the Athabasca River, he met the Reverend Thomas Marsh, an Anglican missionary, and later married Marsh's sister, Ann, of Hay River. He explored the Mackenzie River to the Arctic Ocean, and finally settled on a homestead near Grouard.

W. Fletcher Bredin returned as the Liberal member for Athabasca in 1905; he sat in the Legislature for four years. In 1909 he was defeated by a fellow Liberal, Jean-Léon Coté, and retired from politics. W. Fletcher Bredin contributed much to the development of Northern Alberta. He died December 30, 1942 at Edmonton at the age of 85.

[See: Canadian Who's Who, 1912]

dr. robert george brett

Born November 16, 1851 at Strathroy, Upper Canada, son of James Brett and Catherine Mallon. He was of pioneer Anglican of Anglo-Irish descent. Educated at Strathroy grammar school, he attended the University of Toronto, graduating in Medicine in 1874. Dr. Brett then did post-graduate medical studies at New York, Philadelphia and Vienna. He practiced first at Arkona, Ontario before moving to Winnipeg. Dr. Brett was one of the founders of the University of Manitoba Medical Faculty in 1880 and served on the faculty for six years. In 1886 he established a private hospital at the Banff hot springs where he was senior surgeon for decades.

Dr. Brett returned as the member for Banff (N.W.T.) in 1888. He sat in the Legislative Assembly for thirteen years. He served as President of the Executive Council (premier) from 1888 to 1891 and as a cabinet minister from 1898 to 1901; he resigned his seat in 1901. He was an unsuccessful Conservative candidate for Banff in 1905 and for Cochrane in 1909. He served a term as the president of the Alberta Conservative Association. Prime Minister Robert Borden appointed him the second Lieutenant Governor of Alberta in 1915 and he held this position for ten years. In 1925 he retired from politics at the age of 73. He died September 16, 1929 at Calgary.

[See: Canadian Parliamentary Guide, 1925]

edwin william 'ted' brunsden

Born in 1896 in Kent, England, son of E. Samuel Brunsden and his wife Ellen Scott. He was of English descent and an Anglican He came to Canada, enlisted in the Canadian army and saw active service with the 29th Battalion on the Western Front. After the war, Brunsden attended the Olds Agricultural College, graduating in Science and becoming an agricultural agent at Brooks. In 1957 he was an unsuccessful federal candidate.

'Ted' Brunsden returned as the Progressive Conservative member for the Medicine Hat riding in 1958. He sat in the House of Commons for four years as a private member on the government side of the House. In 1962, he was defeated by the former Social Credit member H.A. 'Bud' Olson. He then retired from politics at the age of 66. He died in 1973.

john charles buckley

Born November 26, 1863 at Enniskerry, County Wicklow, Ireland, son of Henry Buckley and his wife Maria Louise Griffiths. His father had a large estate and he was of Elizabethan Planter stock. He was of Anglo-Irish descent and an Anglican. Educated at Carlow, he managed his father's estate for two decades. He came to Canada in 1906 and farmed in the Gleichan area. He was active in the establishment of the United Farmers of Alberta organization.

J.C. Buckley returned as the UFA member for Gleichen in 1921. He sat in the Legislature as his party's whip for 14 years. In 1935 he was defeated by Social Creditor Isaac M. McCune and retired from politics at the age of 72. In 1884 he had married his cousin Susan Buckley of Enniskerry. They had ten children. His daughter Beatrice 'Bea' Buckley, a teacher, married Humphrey Parlby, the only son of Mary Irene Parley, the UFA member for Lacombe (1921-1935). J.C. Buckley died in February, 1942 at Calgary at the age of 78.

[See: Canadian Parliamentary Guide, 1935]

leighton e. buckwell

Born November 28, 1918 at Fort Macleod, son of Edward Leighton Buckwell and his wife Jeanette Louise Maunsel, both descended from early pioneer families. He was of English descent and an Anglican. He became a prominent Fort Macleod rancher and remained a bachelor.

Leighton E. Buckwell returned as the Social Credit member for Macleod in 1967 and sat in the Legislature for eight years. In 1975 he did not seek re-election and retired from politics.

[See: Canadian Parliamentary Guide, 1975; Who's Who in Southern Alberta, 1988]

ambrose upton gladstone bury, k.c.

Born August 1, 1869 at Doronings House, County Kildare, Ireland, son of Charles Michael Bury and his wife Margaret Aylmer. His mother was a descendent of Baron Matthew Aylmer, Governor-General of Canada from 1831 to 1835. He was of Anglo-Irish descent and an Anglican. He attended Trinity College, Dublin and was admitted to the Irish Bar in 1906. He came to Canada, settling in Edmonton, where he became a prominent lawyer, having been called to the Alberta Bar in 1913. He was named a King's Council member in 1928. Active in civic politics, he served first as an alderman and then as the mayor of the city from 1927 to 1930. He had been an unsuccessful provincial candidate in 1921. He acted as Chancellor of the Diocese of Athabasca for many years.

A.U.G. Bury returned as the Conservative member for the Edmonton East riding in 1925. He was defeated in 1926 but re-elected in 1930. He sat in the House of Commons for a total of six years before he vacated his seat on his appointment as a judge of the Northern Alberta District Court in 1935. He sat on the Bench for nine years. He died in September 1964.

[See: Canadian Who's Who, 1936-37]

C

rev. david john carter, d.d.

Born April 6, 1934 at Moose Jaw, Saskatchewan, son of Archdeacon John Wilfred Carter. He was of English descent and an Anglican. Educated at Regina and Medicine Hat, he attended Mount Royal College, Calgary the University of Manitoba, graduating in Arts (158, St. Johns College, Manitoba for his theological training (L.Th,. 1961, D.D., 1968) and the Anglican Theological College, University of British Columbia (S.T.B., 1968) He was dean of Calgary's Holy Redeemer Cathedral from 1969 to 1979.

David J. Carter returned as the Progressive Conservative member for Calgary Egmont in 1979 and sat in the Legislature for 14 years. In 1986 he was elected by the members of the chamber to be Speaker of the Legislature, a position which he held for seven years. In 1993 he did not seek re-election and retired from politics at the age of 59. In 1998 he was serving as the chief executive officer of Eagle Butte Resource Development at Elk Water near Medicine Hat.

[See: Canadian Who's Who, 1998]

douglas marmaduke **caston**

Born in 1917 at Macklin Saskatchewan, son of John E. Caston and his wife Edna Walker. He was of English descent and an Anglican. During WWII he enlisted in the Royal Canadian Air force and saw active service in western Europe. After the war he became the publisher and general editor of the Edson weekly newspaper.

hugh dt. quentin cayley

Born February 9, 1857 at Toronto, son of the Hon. William Cayley, a lawyer, and his wife Emma. His family was politically involved and his ancestors included the Rev. Edward C. Cayley, an Anglican clergyman. He was of English descent and an Anglican. Educated at Guelph, he attended Upper Canada College and the University of Toronto, graduating in Arts in 1881. He studied the law while working as a journalist. He came to the Territories as a young man and became the editor of The Calgary Herald. In 1886 he was admitted to the Northwest Territories Bar.

Hugh St. Quentin Cayley returned as one of the Calgary members of the Northwest Territories Legislative Council. He returned to the N.W.T. Legislature Assembly and served briefly as the president of the Executive Council in 1893. In 1894 he did not seek re-election. He was a prominent early citizen of the booming community of Calgary. On one occasion his outspokenness resulted in a charge of contempt of court which led to a jail sentence. In 1897 he moved to Vancouver where he practiced law. Twenty years later he became a judge of district court. He died April 13, 1934 at Vancouver at the age of 81.

[See: Who's Who and Why, 1912]

barrie chivers

Born in November of 1940 at Ryley, son of Oswald Chivers and his wife Enid Slee. He was of English descent and an Anglican. Educated at Ryley, he attended the University of Alberta, graduating in Arts and then in Law. He was admitted to the Alberta Bar in 1970. He practiced law in Edmonton in the legal firm of Wright and Chivers. In 1971 he was an unsuccessful provincial candidate.

Barrie Chivers returned as a New Democratic MLA in the Edmonton Strathcona by-election of December 17, 1990. He sat in the Legislature as an Opposition member for two years. In 1993 he was defeated in his re-election bid by Liberal Al Zaiwny, and retired from politics at the age of 50.

[See: Canadian Parliamentary Guide, 1993]

joseph a. clarke

Born September 20, 1869 at Osnabruck, Ontario, son of Captain James Clarke and his wife Margaret Adams. His father had been born in Ireland in 1828 and served as an officer in the British army as a young man. He was of Anglo-Irish descent and an Anglican. As a young man he went to the Klondike in the 1897 gold rush. Later he served with the North West Mounted Police. Educated at Brockville, he attended Toronto's Osgoode Hall Law School before being admitted to the Ontario Bar in 1906. He came to Alberta in 1908 and settled at Edmonton where he practiced law for the next 30 years. In 1911 he married Gwendolen Ashbury, daughter of an Anglican clergyman. Later he referred to himself as a Protestant in religious faith and politically a Liberal with radical views.

Active in civic politics, he served for many years as an alderman and twice as mayor: from 1919 to 1921 and again from 1935 to 1938. He was known was the stormy petrel of Edmonton Civic politics. He was an alderman at the time of his death and was replaced on council by his wife Gwendolen. Joseph A. Clarke was an unsuccessful provincial candidate four times: for Clearwater in 1937 and for Edmonton in 1926, 1930 and in the 1937 by-election. He was prominent in the establishment of the Edmonton Eskimo Football Team; their first field was called Clarke Stadium.

simon john clarke, jr.

Born December 22, 1852, son of Simon John Clarke, a lawyer and French translator, and his wife Catherine Crofton, daughter of Sir Henry Crofton. He was of Anglo-Irish descent and an Anglican. His paternal grandfather, John Clarke (1781-1852), was an employee of the Hudson's Bay Company and Chief Factor at Rocky Mountain House in 1805. After a period as partner of John Jacob Astor of the American Fur Company, by 1821 he was again working for the Hudson's Bay Company as a fur trader. At this time he married Swiss-born Miss Trauclar. Their eldest son, Simon John Clarke, was born at Fort Pelly, Rupert's Land in 1824. He attended McGill University in Montreal. Simon John Clarke, Jr. was educated in the public schools of Quebec. He studied medicine and later referred to himself as 'doctor', although his actual qualifications cannot be confirmed. In 1876, as a young man, he enlisted in the Northwest Mounted Police and served at Fort Walsh during the Sitting Bull crisis and later at Fort Calgary. Following his demobilization from the force in 1882, he settled at Calgary where he served on the first Town council. He became the proprietor of the Calgary Queen's Hotel and a well-known local businessman. He was an unsuccessful N.W.T. Assembly candidate in 1894 and 1898. In 1896 he was an unsuccessful federal candidate for the Alberta riding. He and Lt. Thomas H.B. Cochrane split the southern Alberta vote, allowing the election of Liberal Edmonton publisher, Frank Oliver. Later, after serving as a Calgary commissioner he travelled widely.

In 1991, Prime Minister Robert Borden appointed Dr. Simon John Clarke as superintendent of Rocky Mountain (Banff) Park and he held the position for seven years. He died June 1, 1918 at Rochester Minnesota.

[See: History of Alberta, 1912]

malcolm glen clegg

Born October 2, 1933 at Fairview, he was of English descent and an Anglican. Educated at Fairview, he became a farmer in the area. Active in civic politics he served first as a councilor and then as a reeve in Fairview.

M. Glen Clegg returned as the Progressive Conservative member for Dunvegan in 1986. He was re-elected in 1989, 1993, and 1997. In 1998 he was an unsuccessful candidate for the speakership of the Legislature, losing to Kenneth Kowalski.

[See: Canadian Parliamentary Guide, 1997]

thomas henry belhouse cochrane

Born in 1860 in England, son of Admiral of the Fleet, Sir Thomas Chochrane and grandson of Sir Alexander Cochrane, admiral of the Blue. On February 19, 1887 he married Lady Adela Chevlotte, daughter of John Edward Cornwallis, Earl of Stradbrooke, who had served with the Coldstream Guards at the Battle Waterloo. In 1883 Lt. Cochrane acquired leasehold of a 55 000 acre ranch west of High River where he became one of the most prominent ranchers in Southern Alberta. He constructed a large house at Witford for his bride and three years later became the proprietor of a large lumber mill at Witford. One of his local projects was the building of a narrow gauge railway from Witford to Dogpound which became known as the Grand Valley line. He also started a brickyard and operated a coal mine in Canmore which failed in 1895. By the mid 1890s Witford had become a ghost town.

Interested in politics, Thomas H.B. Cochrane unsuccessfully contested the federal riding of Alberta as a Conservative in 1896. He was defeated by Frank Oliver, the Liberal publisher of The Edmonton Bulletin by a 784 vote margin. After his defeat, he and Lady Cochrane returned to Britain where he re-enlisted in the Royal Navy. From 1899 to 1910 he served as Deputy Governor of the Isle of Wight and later became a naval Rear Admiral. He died March 31, 1925 at Bournemouth, England at the age of 65.

[See: Men of Dawn, 1993]

charles cockroft

Born Mary 20, 1887 at Leeds, England, son of Charles Cockroft and his wife Jane, his grandfather was a successful silk manufacturer. He was of English descent and an Anglican. He emigrated to Canada as a young man in 1906 and became a general merchant in Gadsby. He served as the mayor and also as a school trustee.

Charles Cockroft returned as the Social Credit member for Stettler in 1935. Premier Aberhart took him into his first cabinet as Provincial treasurer and Minister of Municipal affairs. He held this portfolio for two years before being fired by the Premier. He sat in the Legislature for five years. In 1940, he did not seek re-election and retired from politics at the age of 52.

[See: Canadian Who's Who, 1936-37]

charles frederick pringle **conybeare**, q.c.

Born May 19, 1860 at Little Sutton, Middlesex, England, son of Henry C. Conybeare, an eminent engineer, and his wife Ann Newport Moore, daughter of General Moore. His grandfather was Dean W. Daniel Conybeare, a pioneer geologist. He was of English descent and an Anglican. Educated at Westminster public school, he attended the University of Oxford. He came to Canada in 1880, studied law in Winnipeg, and was admitted to the Northwest Territories Bar in 1885. He settled in Lethbridge where he was a legal partner of W. Carlos Ives. For a time he served as president of the Alberta Law Society. He was an unsuccessful territorial candidate in 1887.

Bishop's College, Lennoxville, PQ, granted Conybreare an honorary Doctor of Laws degree. He also served as Chancellor of the diocese of Calgary for many years. In addition, Carles Conybeare was a poet; his published works include Vahn Fried (Toronto 1903) and Lyrics from the West (Toronto, 1907). He died July 31, 1927 at Lethbridge at the age of 67.

ashley horace cholwel h. cooper

Born February 6, 1905 at Vermilion, Alberta, son of Sextus R.P. Cooper and his wife Myrthle Harrower. He was of Anglo-Irish descent and an Anglican. He was related to Major Sir Patrick Ashley Cooper (1887-1916), a governor of the Hudson's Bay Company and a director of the Bank of England. He attended the Camrose Normal School graduating with a teaching certificate. He then taught for a number of years in rural Alberta schools. Later he became the publisher and managing editor of he Vermilion Standard, a weekly newspaper. He held this position for thirty years.

Ashley Cooper returned as the Social Credit member for Vermilion in 1955. He sat in the Legislature for the next 20 years. After 1971 he was an opposition member. In 1975 he did not seek re-election and retired from politics at the age of 70.

[See: Canadian Parliamentary Guide, 1970]

william r. cornish

Born March 2, 1890 in Devon, England, son of John Henry Cornish and his wife Mary Louis Rossiter. He was of ethnic English descent and an Anglican. His surname most likely indicated that one of his ancestors had moved from Cornwall to neighbouring Devonshire and was then called a Cornish-man. Educated at Kingsbridge Grammar School, he came to Canada as a young man in 1911, and became a homesteader in the Vermilion district as a late Barr Colonist. Later he became a prominent farmer and sheep breeder.

William R. Cornish returned as the Social Credit member for Vermilion in 1944. He sat in the Legislature for 15 years as a private member on the government side of the chamber. In 1959 he did not seek re-election retiring from politics at the age of 65.

[See: Canadian Parliamentary Guide, 1954]

john robert **cowell**

Born March 6, 1849 at Liverpool England, son of Robert and Emma Cowell. He was of English descent and an Anglican. He was educated privately at Ramsey, Isle of Man. He sat for 20 years as a member of the unique Isle of Man Parliament, the House of Keyn, which was established by the Norsemen in the 11th century. In 1902 he came to the Northwest Territories and settled at Edmonton.

John R. Cowell was appointed as the first Clerk of the Alberta Legislature in 1906 and held position for 17 years. In 1923 he retired at the age of 72.

[See: Who's Who and Why, 1912]

w. dixon craig

Born c.1857 at Toronto, Ontario, son of Thomas Dixon Craig and his wife Annie Crivin. His father served as the Conservative member for the Durham East (Ontario) riding from 1891 to 1900. He was an Anglican. Educated at Toronto, he attended the University of Toronto, qualifying as an engineer in 1899. He worked as an engineer for 14 years in eastern Canada. He came to Alberta in 1913 settling at Edmonton where he studied law and was admitted to the Alberta Bar in 1917. He practiced law in Edmonton as a partner in the legal firm of Woods, Sheery.

W. Dixon Craig served as Chancellor of the Edmonton diocese from 1934 to 1941.

[See: The Canadian Directory of Parliament 1867-1967, 1968]

a. ernest cross

Born June 26, 1861 at Montreal, son of Judge Alexander Cross of the Quebec Court of Queen's Bench and his wife Julie Lunn. He was of English descent and an Anglican. Educated at Haileybury public school at Hertford, England and the Ontario Agricultural College at Guelph, Ont. He came to Alberta in 1884 and became a Calgary brewer and rancher.

In 1899 A. Ernest Cross returned as the member for East Calgary in the Northwest Territories Legislative Assembly where he sat for four years. In 1902 he did not seek re-election and retired from politics. In 1899 he was married to Helen Rothney Macleod, daughter of Colonel James F. Macleod in Calgary's Anglican Cathedral of the Holy Reddemer by bishop Cyprian Pinkham. In 1912 A. Ernest Cross, along with 'Pat' Burns (later Senator Burns), George Lan and A. J. McLean, was a financial backer of the first Calgary Stampede. He died March 19, 1932 at Calgary at the age of 70.

[See: Who's Who and Why, 1912; Alberta and Present, 1924]

douglas george leonard cunnington, mc

Born April 20, 1885 at Bridgenorth, England, son of George Henry Cunnington and his wife Emily Louise Mackney. His father was headmaster of the 'Blue Coat' private school. He was of English descent and an Anglican. Educated at the Blue Coat school, he then spent five years in British Guyana working on a sugar plantation. He came to Alberta in 1910 and purchased a dairy farm near Calgary which he operated for a number of years. At the outbreak of WWI, he enlisted in the Canadian army as a private, but soon received as commission. He went overseas with the Canadian Expeditionary Force and saw active service with the 59th Battalion on the Western Front. In August 1918 he was awarded the Militia Cross for his part in an action at Hallu, France. He had led his platoon forward into machine gun fire to capture a German position. The following day he had received a serious chest wound and was left to die on the battle field. Two months later he had turned up in a German Military Hospital. Returning to Calgary after the war, Cunnington worked for The Calgary Herald for seven years before becoming a prominent businessman and successful investment dealer. In 1934 he was elected as a city alderman and served on the city council for six years.

Interested in federal politics, Col. Douglas George L. Cunnington was nominated as the Conservative candidate to contest the Calgary West by-election, caused by the resignation of R.B. Bennett, the former Prime Minister. He was elected by acclamation on September 18, 1939. He sat in the House of Commons as a private member on the opposition benches for only one afternoon. This is still a record for the shortest term of service in the House. Following the speech from the throne, the Prime Minister rose to announce the general election and Col. Cunnington was defeated at the polls in the March 16, 1940 federal election by Liberal Manley Justin Edwards with a 403 vote margin. He died May 5, 1973 at Calgary at the age of 88.

[See: Parliamentary Guide, 1990]

d

donald watson **davis**

Born November 3, 1849 in Windham County, on a farm near Londonderry, Vermont, U.S.A., son of Daniel W. Davis and his wife Laura. He was of Anglo-Irish descent. The state census of 1860 lists him as a "farm laborer" at the age of 11. In 1865 he enlisted in the Union army and he saw active service during the final months of the American Civil War. Two years later he enlisted in the American Army where he served as an active quartermaster sergeant with the 13th United States Infantry at Fort Shaw, Monata Territories. In 1870 he took part in a raid on a Peigan encampment. In 1871 he was demobilized and became an agent for the I.G. Baker Company. By 1873 he was with J.J. Healty as a whisky trader working out of Fort Whoop-Up (or Fort Hamilton on the Oldman River near the site of the present city of Lethbridge.) Davis moved to Fort Macleod where he worked as a carpenter. Later he again became an agent for the I.G. Baker Company and managed the firm's Fort Macleod store. Taciturn and close-mouthed concerning his army life and his dealings as a whisky trader, he became a prominent citizen. His reformation was completed when he became an Anglican. In December 1886 he applied to become a British subject; his papers were signed by James F. Macleod, Magistrate. In 1887, he married Lily Elizabeth Josephine Grier, a Fort Macleod school teacher and sister of David Johnston Grier, a former member of the Northwest Mounted Police who became Mayor of Fort Macleod and was a wealthy rancher in the area. It was on his honeymoon that he filed the nomination paper for his candidacy as the first Member of Parliament to be returned from the District of Alberta, Northwest Territories.

donald watson **davis** (cont'd)

D. W. Davis returned as the Conservative member for the new Alberta riding in 1888. He sat in the House of Commons for nine years until he vacated his seat on being appointed chief federal customs officer for the remote Yukon Territory in 1896. On his arrival at Fort Cudahy, the Northwest Mounted Police post, he met John J. Healy for whom he had worked in the old days of Fort Whoop-Up. Davis had wanted to go to an isolated place in the 'out-back'. However, civilization followed him with the Klondike Gold Rush of '98. Dawson City changed from a remote outpost to a city of 20 000 miners and gold seekers in a matter of months. The collector of customs was the most prominent government official in residence at the boom town. On June 2, 1902 he resigned from the civil service and became a gold miner. He died June 6, 1906 at Dawson City; his funeral service was held at St. Paul's Anglican church. He was only 53.

[See: Canadian Parliamentary Guide, 1889]

frederick 'fred' davis

Born May 26, 1868 at Mitchell, Ontario, son of W. R. Davis. His father was the publisher and managing editor of The Mitchell Advocate for 58 years. He was of English descent and an Anglican. While a young man he served as the mayor of Mitchell. He moved to the Northwest Territories, settled at Calgary and later became a farmer in the Gleichen area and the proprietor of a knitting factory.

'Fred' Davis returned as the Independent member for Gleichen in 1917. He sat in the Legislature for four years on the opposition benches. In 1921 he did not seek re-election. Turning to federal politics, Davis returned as the Independent member for the Calgary East riding in 1925. He sat in the House of Commons for one year. In 1926 he was defeated by Liberal H. B. Adshead, and retired from politics at the age of 58.

dr. leverett george de veber

Born February 10, 1849 at St. John, New Brunswick, son of Richard Sandys De Veber and his wife Caroline Beer, daughter of a British naval captain. He was of English descent and an Anglican. His great-grandfather, Col. Gabriel De Veber had served in the British army during the rebellion of the American colonies. After the war he moved north to New Brunswick. George De Veber was educated at Windsor, Nova Scotia; Bartholomew's Hospital, London, England and the University of Pennsylvania, graduating in Medicine. He practiced his profession in Lethbridge.

George De Veber was elected as the Liberal member for Lethbridge in the Northwest Territorial Council in the general elections of 1898 and 1902. He served as the government whip in the Assembly. On the creation of the Province of Alberta, he entered the cabinet as Minister Without Portfolio, but resigned on being called to the Senate in 1906.

[See: Who's Who and Why, 1910]

edgar dewney

Born November 5, 1835 at Bideford, Devonshire, England, son of Charles Dewney and his wife Fanny Hollingshead. He was of English descent and an Anglican. Educated at Exeter, he qualified as a civil engineer and land surveyor at Cardiff, Wales. He came to British Columbia colony in 1859 where, through the influence of the British Colonial Secretary, Sir Bulwer Lytton, he was hired to survey the site of New Westminster.

Edgar Dewney sat in the colony's Legislature as the Conservative member for the Kootenay riding from 1869, and after it joined Confederation he returned as the Conservative member for Yale in 1872. He sat in the House of Commons for nine years as a strong supporter of Sir John A. Macdonald's government and the construction of the railway from Central Canada to Vancouver. He resigned his seat when he was appointed as the fifth Lieutenant Governor of the Northwest Territories in 1881. His careful handling of the situation following the 1885 Northwest Rebellion was partly responsible for preventing any further revolts in the Canadian provinces. Dewney resigned as Lieutenant Governor in 1888. He was re-elected to the House of Commons and taken into Prime Minister Macdonald's cabinet as Minister of the Interior; he held this portfolio for four years. He vacated his seat in the Commons in October 1892 on his appointment as the Lieutenant Governor of British Columbia. He held this vice-regal post for a five-term. In 1897 Edgar Dewney retired from politics at the age of 62. He died August 8, 1916 at Victoria.

[See: Canadian Who's Who, 1912]

58 james 'jim' dinning

Born December 4, 1952 at Edmonton, son of John B. Dinning and his wife Frances. He was of Anglo-Irish descent and an Anglican. His ancestors came from Country Armagh, Ireland. Matthew Dinning (1843-1892) settled at Strathroy, Ontario where he became a farmer. His grandson, Robert John Dinning was a bank manager who moved to Alberta as manager of several branches of the Merchants Back of Canada. In 1924 R.J. Dinning was appointed as Commissioner of the Alberta Liquor Control Board by the Cabinet. His grandson, 'Jim' Dinning attended Queen's University, and in 1974 married Jane Ursula Peacock, daughter of Frederick H. Peacock, Minister for Industry and Commerce in the Lougheed cabinet at the time. A provincial civil servant, he became the deputy minister of Federal and Intergovernmental Affairs in early 1980.

'Jim' Dinning returned as the Progressive Conservative member for Calgary Shaw in 1986. He sat in the Legislature for 11 years serving as the Minister of Community and Occupational Health in 1986, the Minister of Education in 1988 under Premier Getty, and the Provincial Treasurer from 1992 to 1997 under Premier Klein. In 1997, he did not seek re-election and retired from politics at the age 44.

[See: Canadian Who's Who, 1997]

mary julia dover (neé cross), o.b.e, o.c.

Born in 1905 at Calgary, Alberta, daughter of A. Ernest Cross and his wife Helen 'Nellie' Macleod. She was named after her grandmother Mary Macleod. Her maternal grandfather was Col. James F. Macleod. In 1930 she married Mel Dover who had been a fighter pilot in WWI. Shortly after their marriage the Dover family moved to Bombay, India where Mel Dover was manager of the Ford automobile dealership. In 1939, they returned to Calgary where May Dover enlisted in the Canadian Women's Army Corps and became the commanding officer of Military District 13. In December 1942 she was posted overseas to London. A year later she returned to Canada on her appointment as Colonel of the C.W.A.C. camp at Kitchener, Ontario. She was the highest ranking officer of the Canadian Women's Army Corps. In 1946, she was awarded the Order of the British Empire in recognition of her service. Mary Dover returned to Calgary following her demobilization and became active in politics. She served as a Calgary alderman from 1948 to 1952 and again from 1957 to 1960. She was an unsuccessful provincial Liberal candidate for Calgary in 1948 and again in 1955. Late in life, she became resident of Midnapore, Calgary. She died in her nineties.

[See: Braehead, 1986]

robert wagner dowling

Born September 25, 1924 at Camrose, son of Harold James Dowling and his wife Emma. He was of English descent and an Anglican. He was educated at Camrose. During WWII he enlisted in the Royal Canadian Air Force and saw active service as a flying officer in Europe. After the war he attended the University of British Columbia, graduating in Arts and the University of Alberta, graduating in Science. He became a pharmacist at Jasper.

Robert W. 'Bob' Dowling returned as the Progressive Conservative member for Edson in the October 28, 1969 by-election defeating Grant Notley, the Alberta New Democratic party leader. He sat in the Legislature for ten years. In 1971 Premier Lougheed appointed him to the cabinet as the Minister of Consumer and Corporate Affairs. In 1979 he did not seek re-election and retired from politics at the age of 50.

[See: Canadian Parliamentary Guide, 1975]

lawrence ernest oscar duke

Born December 21, 1880 at Mono Mills, Ontario, son of William Duke and his wife Mary Ann Speers. He was of Anglo-Irish descent and an Anglican. Educated at Orangeville, Ontario, he attended the Calgary Normal School, qualifying as a teacher. In 1908 he married Agnes Jackson, his childhood sweetheart. They served for three years as Anglican missionaries at Moose Factory, James Bay. Later he became a teacher at Camrose.

L.E. Oscar Duke returned as the Social Credit member for the Rocky Mountain constituency in 1935. It was a large constituency extending from the American border to north of Rocky Mountain House. In 1940 he was re-elected as the Social Credit member for the newly formed Pincher Cree-Crowsnest constituency. He sat in the Legislature as a government back bencher for 14 years. In 1949 he did not seek re-election and retired from politics at the age of 68. He died March 5, 1956.

[See: Canadian Parliamentary Guide, 1949]

e

robert barry eaton

Born August 5, 1871 at Truro, Nova Scotia, son of James K. Eaton, Canadian Engineer, and A.K. Petblado. He was of English descent and an Anglican. He was educated at Truro. During the South African war, he served with the Southern Constabulary and remained with it after the war. As a young man he came to the Northwest Territories and homesteaded in the Craigmyle district in 1904. He became a well-known famer in addition to operating a fox farm.

Robert B. Eaton returned as the Liberal member for Hand Hills in 1913. He sat in the Chamber as a government back bencher for eight years. In 1921 he was defeated in the bed for re-election by UFA candidate George Foster and retired from politics at the age of 50. During WWII he served overseas seeing active service on the Western Front. He rose to the rank of colonel. In 1935 Col. Eaton retired to Chilliwack, BC.

[See: Canadian Parliamentary Guide, 1921]

sheila barbara embury

Born June 6, 1931 at Calgary, daughter of Herbert L. Pease and his wife Beatrice M. Tuffler. She was of English descent and an Anglican. Educated at Calgary, she became a nurse and then attended the University of Calgary. She became a professor of Nursing at the University of Alberta and served on the board of directors of the Alberta Housing Corporation prior to becoming active in politics.

Sheila Embury returned as the Progressive Conservative member for Calgary North West in 1979. She sat in the Legislature for seven years. In 1986 she did not seek re-election and retired from politics at the age of 48.

[See: Canadian Parliamentary Guide, 1986]

f

frank john williams **fane**, m.c.

Born February 23, 1897 on the Beaver Lake family farm southeast of Edmonton, son of Frank W. Fane and his wife Margaret Duff. He was of English/Scottish descent and an Anglican. Educated at Beaver Lake, Vegreville and Camrose, he attended the University of Alberta and became a famer in the Vegreville area. He was active in civic politics serving as a municipal councilor and as chairman of the school board. He rose to the rank of major in the CASF and reserve army. He was an unsuccessful federal candidate in 1940 and again in 1957.

Frank J. W. Fane returned as the Progressive Conservative member for the Vegreville riding in 1958. He sat in the House of Commons for 11 years. In 1968 he did not seek re-election and retired from politics at the age of 70.

[See: Canadian Parliamentary Guide, 1968]

hugh craig farthing, k.c.

Born July 18, 1892 at Montreal, son of the Right Reverend John C. Farthing, Anglican bishop of Montreal, and his wife Elizabeth May Kemp. He was of English descent and of United Empire Loyalist stock. Educated at Kingston, he attended McGill University in Montreal and then Osgoode Law School in Toronto. During WWII he went overseas with the Canadian Expeditionary Force and saw active service as an officer on the Western Front. After the war he practiced law in Toronto and then moved to Calgary where he became a prominent Conservative.

Hugh C. Fathering returned as the Conservative member for the multi-member Calgary constituency in 1930. He sat in the Legislature as an opposition member for five years. In 1935, he failed in his bid for re-election and returned to his law practice. In 1958 the Justice Minister appointed H.C. Farthing as a judge of the Alberta District Court. Two years later he was elevated to the Alberta Supreme Court: Trial Division. He served as the Chancellor of the diocese of Calgary from 1946 to 1964. He retired from the Bench in 1967 and died June 8, 1968 in Calgary at the age of 76.

[See: Canadian Who's Who, 1936-37]

frank ford, k.c.

Born March 4, 1873 at Toronto, Ontario. He was of English descent and an Anglican. Educated at Toronto's Ontario Academy, he attended the University of Toronto, graduating in Civil Law. He was admitted to the Ontario Bar in 1895. He then became the private secretary of D'Alton McCarthy (1836-1898), long-time of parliament for the Simcoe North riding who headed the 'Equal Rights' movement, and then the private secretary of Ontario Premier Arthur S. Hardy. While working in the civil service (Ontario Treasurer's Department) he returned to the University of Toronto where he received a doctorate in law in 1909. Moving to Saskatchewan in 1906, he served as the province's first deputy Attorney General. Four years later he came to Alberta where he became a prominent Edmonton lawyer with the legal firm of Emery, Newell and Ford. Frank Ford had the distinction of creating a King's Counsel in three provinces: Saskatchewan in 1907, Ontario in 1910 and Alberta in 1913.

Frank K. Ford was appointed as Justice of the Alberta Supreme Court: Trial Dvision by Justice Minister Ernest Lapointe in 1926. Ten years later he was elevated to the Appellate Division. He vacated his seat on the Bench in 1954 at the age of 81. Justice Ford served as Chancellor of the Anglican diocese of Edmonton from 1922 to 1933 and again from 1942 to 1961. He died March 21, 1965 at Edmonton.

[See: Alberta Judicial Biographical Dictionary, 1990]

g

annie gale

Born in 1879 at Dudley, Worchestershire, England. She was of English descent and an Anglican. She was educated at a Dudley private school for young ladies. In 1901 she married John Gale, a civil engineer. They came to Canada in 1912 settling at Calgary where her husband practiced his profession. Mrs. Gale became an active social reformer as a member of the Consumers' League which established a municipal market. Later she was the leader in force behind the Vacant Lots Garden Clubs. By 1915 there were 2 000 lots under cultivation by 1 125 individuals, growing vegetables. Two years later there were 6 000 lots. She was also the president of St. Mark's Anglican Church Women's Club. In 1917 Mrs. Gale returned as the first woman to serve as a Calgary alderman. She was an unsuccessful provincial candidate in the election of 1921. She served for sixty years on the city council and two on the public school board. In 1925 she and her husband moved to Vancouver. She died in 1970 in West Vancouver.

[See: Citymarkers: Calgarians After the Frontier, 1987]

james gladstone

Born May 21, 1887 near Mountain Hill, district of Alberta, Northwest Territories, son of a Blood Chief. He was an Anglican. He was educated at St. Paul's Anglican Missionary School on the Blood Reserve, he attended the Calgary Indian Industrial School. He was a cowboy, R.N.W.M.P. scout and a mail courier before he became a small rancher and farmer on the Blood Reserve in 1920. From 1949 to 1957 he was the president of the Alberta Indian Association, and in 1957 he was named as the association's honorary president.

James Gladstone was summoned to the Canadian Senate by Prime Minister John Diefenbaker on January 31, 1958, becoming the first native-born senator in Canadian history. The Blackfoot language was his native tongue and he used it in the Senate. At the time of Gladstone's appointment it was discovered that he did not fulfill the financial requirements in order to take up his seat, whereupon some of his friends came to his rescue.

[See Canadian Who's Who, 1967]

george wellington greene

Born June 5, 1862 at Athens, Upper Canada, son of William Greene and his wife Mary Webster. He was of English descent and an Anglican. Educated at Athens, he studied law with C.F. Fraser, later Ontario Minister of Public Works. He attended Toronto's Osgoode Law School and was admitted to the Ontario Bar in 1887. He first practiced law at Athens, but in 1892 he came to the Northwest Territories, settling permanently at Red Deer where he became prominent lawyer in the legal firm of Green and Payne. In 1898 he was an unsuccessful candidate for the N.W.T. Legislative Assembly. When Red Deer became a town in 1901, George Green became the town solicitor.

Justice Minister C.J. Doherty appointed G.W. Green as judge of the Medicine Hat Court in 1915. When the courts were reorganized in 1935, he was transferred to the Southern Alberta District Court. He died July 14, 1936 while on a family visit at Athabasca. He was 74.

[See: Canadian Who's Who, 1936]

john johnson gregory

Born c. 1940 in the Niagara district of Upper Canada. He was of United Empire Loyalist stock and an Anglican. Educated at St. Catharines, Ontario, he became a prosperous local farmer. Active in community affairs, he filled various municipal offices, including reeve of the Niagara district. In 1884 he moved to North Bay, Ontario where he farmed and also served as the reeve. He came to the district of Alberta, NWT in 1893 where he homesteaded near Lacombe. He became a wealthy and prominent farmer and was active in the establishment of the town of Lacombe. A life-long militia supporter, he entered the volunteer militia at the age of 16. He joined the St. Catharine's troop cavalry in 1857. Lt. Gregory saw active service during the Trent affair and the Fenian Raids of 1866. In June 1883 he was promoted to lieutenant colonel. Interested in politics John J. Gregory unsuccessfully contested the riding of Strathcona in the federal election of 1904. At the time, he stated that he desired the fullest measure of provincial autonomy for Alberta, with the right to determine their own school programs and administer their own resources. He died c. 1911 at Lacombe.

[See: Who's Who and Why, 1912]

74 william antrobus **griesbach**, g.s.o.

Born January 3, 1878 at Fort Qu'Appelle, Northwest Territories, son of Major Henry Griesbach and his wife Emma Hodgins. As a young man his father had served in the Prussian army and on coming to Canada in 1874, was the first man to enlist in the newly formed Northwest Mounted Police. He was of German/English descent and an Anglican. Educated at Winnipeg's St. John College, he qualified as a lawyer. At the outbreak of the South African War (Boer War) he enlisted and saw action with the Canadian Mounted Rifles. After being demobilized he was admitted to the N.W.T. Bar in 1901 and practiced law in Edmonton, becoming the senior partner in the firm Griesbach, O'Connor (Q.V.) and O'Connor (Q.V.). While still in his twenties he served as mayor of Edmonton. He was an unsuccessful provincial candidate in 1905 and again in 1913. During WWI he served in the Canadian Expeditionary Force on the Western Front where he was awarded the D.S.O. in 1916 and rose to the rank of brigadier-general. After the war he became the inspector-general of the Canadian Army for Western Canada, with the rank of major-general.

Major-general W. A. Griesbach returned as the Unionist Pro-Government member for the Edmonton West riding in 1917, defeating Liberal incumbent Frank Oliver with the aid of the overseas soldiers' vote. He sat in the House of Commons for one term until his appointment to the Senate in 1921. He was an active senator until his death on January 21, 1945 at Ottawa at the age of 67.

[See: Canadian Who's Who, 1938; Canadian Parliamentary Companion, 1944] h

richard **hardisty**, sr.

Born c. 1788 at London, England. He was of English descent and an Anglican. As a young man, he enlisted in the British army and saw active service in Willington's army and infantry regiment in the Peninsula War and the battle of Waterloo in June 1815. He came to North America in 1817 and became an indentured employee of the Hudson's Bay Company. During his five-year contract he served in the company's Sastmarin fur trading post. Over the years, he served in various places and rose to become a chief trader in 1936 at Lake Nipissing. In time he became Chief Factor. In 1821 he married Marguerite, daughter of Chief Trader of the Hudson's Bay Company, James Sutherland, and his indigenous wife, 'à la façon du pays'. They had six sons and four daughters. All the sons became employees of the Hudson's Bay Company: William Lucas Hardisty (1822-1881) was a factor at Ford Laird and later Chief Factor of the Mackenzie River District; Richard Charles Hardisty (1832-1889) was Chief Factor at Ford Edmonton and died as a Canadian Senator; Joseph, George, Henry and Thomas. The daughter of his eldest son, 'Bella' Hardisty, married James Alexander Lougheed in 1884. [See: E. Peter Lougheed] The eldest daughter of Richard Hardisty, Isabella Sophia Hardistry (d. November 18, 1913), married Donald Alexander Smith (1820-1914), Chief Factor of the Hudson's Bay Company and later Baron Strathcona and Mount Royal. They had one daughter, Margaret Charlotte Smith, who in accordance with the special remainder, succeeded to her father's title. The fourth son of Richard Hardisty, Richard Charles Hardisty (1832-1889) was the Hudson's Bay Company Chief Factor of the Upper Saskatchewan District, stationed at Fort Edmonton for 17 years. In 1866, he married Eliza, daughter of George Milward McDougall, Methodist Morley Missionary.

He was an unsuccessful federal candidate for the Alberta riding in 1887. Prime Minister Sir John A. Macdonald summoned Hardisty to the Senate in 1888.

[See: Senator Hartisty's Praries 1849-1889, 1978]

graham isle harle

Born December 9, 1931 at Newcastle-upon-Tyne, England, son of James A. Harle and his wife Constance Balfour. He was of English descent and an Anglican. Educated at Durham and Uttoxeter, England and Edmonton, he attended the University of Alberta, graduating in Law. He was admitted to the Alberta Bar and practiced law in Stettler.

Graham Harle returned as the Progressive Conservative member in February 13, 1972 in the Stettler by-election and sat in the Legislature for 14 years. He served as the Minister of Consumer and Corporate Affairs in 1975 and then as Solicitor General in 1979. He resigned from the cabinet on November 16, 1983. In 1986 he did not seek re-election and retired from politics at the age of 54.

[See: Canadian Parliamentary Guide, 1986]

robert henry charles harrison

Born July 30, 1902 at Edmonton, son of Dr. John Darley Harrison and Annie Laura Robertson. His father was a pioneer physician, arriving in Edmonton in 1896. He was an Anglican. Educated at Edmonton Trinity College School in Port Hope, Ontario, he attended the University of Alberta, graduating with a law degree in 1926. He then articled with H. Ray Milner of Edmonton and was admitted to the Alberta Bar in 1927. He practiced his profession in Leduc and Edmonton for the next 13 years. During WWII he enlisted in the Royal Canadian Air Force rising to the rank of wing commander.

Interested in federal politics, R.H.C. Harrison, running as a Liberal, unsuccessfully contested the Wetaskiwin riding in the 1945 general election. Returning to the practice of law with Charles Grant of Edmonton, he was awarded a K.C. in 1947. He moved to Calgary and became the counsel for Western Canada of B.A. Oil Company. In the 1950s Harrison was a prominent oil company executive and president of the Canadian Petroleum Association. He died in 1970.

james **hartley**

Born November 10, 1888 at Bingley, Yorkshire, England, son of John T. Hartley and his wife Martha Anderton. He was of English descent and an Anglican. Coming to Alberta was a young man in 1906, he became a butcher in Fort Macleod and later a small rancher. During WWI, Hartley saw active service as an officer in the Canadian Army Service Corps on the Western Front.

James Hartley returned as the Social Credit member for Macleod in 1935. He sat in the Legislature for 32 years serving as Deputy Speaker from 1944 to 1955. Premier Manning appointed Hartley as the Minister of Public Works in 1955. He held this cabinet post until 1962. In 1967 Hartley did not seek re-election, and retired from politics at the age of 79.

[See: Canadian Parliamentary Guide, 1966]

horace **harvey**, q.c.

Born in 1863 in Elgin County, Ontario, son of William Harvey and his wife. His father was a Member of Parliament for East Elgin in the 1870s. He was an Anglican. He attended the University of Toronto, graduating first in Arts and then in Law in 1888, he was admitted to the Ontario Bar in 1889. Coming west, he settled in Calgary and was admitted to the N.W.T. Bar in 1893. He practiced law in Calgary. Harvey joined the federal civil service and was named Registrar of Lands Titles for Southern Alberta in 1899 and then Depute Attorney General for the N.W.T. a year later. In 1904 Harvey was appointed a N.W.T. Justice. In 1907 he was transferred to the newly established Alberta Supreme Court as a justice. In 1910 he became the Chief Justice of Alberta, holding this position for 11 years. When the courts were reorganized by acting Justice Minister R.B. Bennett, Harvey became the Chief Justice of the Alberta Supreme Court. This took place in 1924 on the death of Chief Justice David Scott. Horace Harvey, for a second time, became the Chief Justice of Alberta. He was still on the bench when he died in 1949 at the age of 86. He was the last link with the Northwest Territories administration.

[See: Canadian Who's Who, 1948]

ethel vera c. hattersley (née chambers)

Born c. at Belfast, Northern Ireland. She was an Anglican. In 1930, she married Charles Marshall Hattersley, a prominent member of the British Social Credit League. She also became active in the movement. She came to Canada in the early 1950s, settled at Edmonton and became active in the Alberta Social Credit League. She was an unsuccessful provincial candidate for the Social Credit Party in 1955.

[See: Alberta Election Results 1882-1992, 1993]

rev. john martin hattersley, q.c.

Born November 10, 1932 at Swinton Yorkshire England, son of Charles Marshall Hattersley and his wife Ethel Vera Chambers. His father was a personal friend of Major C.H. 'Social Credit' Douglas. He is of ethnic English descent and an Anglican. Educated at Repton Public School, he attended Cambridge University, graduating in Economics and then in Law. Called up for National Service in the British Army, he served as an artillery officer. He emigrated to Canada in 1956, setting at Edmonton where he articled with Ronald Marland of Milner, Steer. He was admitted to the Alberta Bar in 1957, established his law practice in Edmonton and created a Q.C. in 1981.

Strongly committed to the Social Credit movement, he served as personal secretary to Robert H. Thompson, national leader of the Social Credit party and Member of Parliament for the Red Deer Riding from 1962 to 1964. Later Hattersley served as national president of the Social Credit Party from 1973 to 1978. He was an unsuccessful federal candidate for the party in 1972 and again in 1973; he served as the national leader of the Social Credit party from 1980 to 1983. Parallel with his practice of law and his political interest, Martin Hattersley studied and was ordained to the Anglican priesthood. He served as a priest in Edmonton's Anglican Church for St. Peter from 1974 to 1988.

[See: Canadian Who's Who, 1998]

sir frederick william gordon haultain, k.c.

Born November 25, 1857 at Woolwich, England, son of Lieutenant-colonel Frederick Haultain, British artillery officer, and his wife. He was of ethnic English descent and an Anglican. He came to Canada as a child and was educated at Peterborough, Ont. He then attended the University of Toronto, graduating in Classics (B.A. 1879) and then law. He was admitted to the Ontario Bar in 1882 and then Northwest Territories Bar in 1884. He settled at Fort Macleod where he became a prominent lawyer. He was active in Executive Council from 1897 to 1905. He also served as Minister of Education and Attorney General. In 1905, after the provinces of Alberta and Saskatchewan were established, he returned to the Saskatchewan Legislature as the member for Qu'Appelle and sat as the Leader of the Opposition for seven years. Justice Minister C.J. Doherty appointed Haultain as Chief Justice of Saskatchewan in 1912, a position he held for 25 years. In 1916 he was awarded a knighthood by King George V. In 1938 he retired from the Bench at the age of 80 and died January 30, 1942 at Montreal.

[See: Macmillan Dictionary of Biography, 1978]

george hoadley

Born May 16, 1866 at Wetherall, England, son of George Hoadley and his wife Anne Richardson. He was of English descent and an Anglican. Two of his ancestors had been prominent churchmen in the Archbishop of Armagh. George Hoadley was educated at Carlisle grammar school and St. Bees College. He came to Canada as young man in 1891, and in 1900 married Lily Rowles of Okotoks. He operated as a rancher in the High River district. He was an unsuccessful provincial candidate in 1905.

George Hadley returned as the Conservative member for Okotoks in 1909 and sat in the Legislature for 26 years. In 1921 he returned as the UFA member for Okotoks and served as the Minister of Agriculture (1921-1935), Minister of Health and Minister of Railways and Telephones (1934-1935) under Premier R.G. Reid. In 1935 he was defeated by Social Creditor, Rev. William Morrison, a United Church minister. He retired from politics at the age of 69 and died in 1955.

[See: Canadian Who's Who, 1936-37]

john williams hugill, k.c.

Born October 1, 1881 at West Harpool, Durham, England, son of J.H. Hugill and Hannah Hebron. On his maternal side, he descended from Quaker stock. He was of English ethnic descent and an Anglican. Educated at London, England, he came to Canada in 1896 attending Halifax's King's College. Subsequently, he attended the Universities of Manitoba and Alberta where he read law with R.B. Bennett in Calgary. He was admitted to the Alberta and Saskatchewan Bars in 1910 and the British Columbia Bar in 1920. He became a prominent Calgary lawyer in the legal firm of Hugill of O'Keefe. Active in civic politics, he served as an alderman in 1921 and 1922.

Although Hugill was not a Social Credit politician, William Aberhart, the party leader, persuaded him to run as a party candidate on the understanding that he would be appointed as Attorney General if Social Credit formed the government. Hugill returned for the party as a member for Calgary in 1935 and sat in the Legislature for five years. He served as Attorney General for two years before Premier Aberhart fired him. Hugill then crossed the floor of the chamber and sat as an Independent. In 1940, he did not seek re-election and retired from politics at the age of 39.

[See: Canadian Who's Who , 1936-37]

alan william hyland

Born July 28, 1945 at Medicine Hat, son of Ronald Newton Francis Hyland and his wife Doris Laura Childs. He was of English descent and an Anglican. Educated at Senator Gershaw School, Bow Island, he became a farmer. He was active in civic politics and served as a municipal town councilor form 1970 to 1975 and on the executive of the Southern Alberta Regions Alberta Hospitals Association from 1973 to 1975.

Alan Hyland returned as the Progressive Conservative member for Cypress in 1975 and sat in the Legislature as a government backbencher for 18 years. In 1993 he did not seek re-election and retired from politics at the age of 48.

[See: Canadian Parliamentary Guide, 1993]

james duncan hyndman

Born July 29, 1874 at Charlottetown, P.E.I., son of Charles Augustus Hyndman and Catherine Macdonald. He was of English/Scottish descent and an Anglican. Educated at Charlottetown's Prince of Wales College, he read law with A.A. McLean K.C. who served as the federal member for Queens. He was admitted to the P.E.I. Bar in 1899. In the same year, James Hyndman went to Manitoba where he joined his uncle to form a legal firm of Hyndman and Hyndman. He served as a city alderman from 1905 to 1914. Active in federal politics, he was an unsuccessful Conservative candidate for the Edmonton riding in 1908. Turning to provincial politics, he was an unsuccessful Conservative candidate for the Sturgeon constituency in 1913.

Justice Minister C.J. Doherty appointed James D. Hyndman as a Justice of the Alberta Supreme Court in 1914. In 1921 when the courts were reorganized, he was transferred to the Alberta Supreme Court: Appellate Division. He retired from the Bench in 1931. In 1902 he had married Ethel Davis, daughter of Sir Louis Davies, a former premier of Prince Edward Island and a Chief Justice of Cnaada. Two of J.D. Hyndman's grandsons became prominent in provincial politics: L.D. 'Lou' Hyndman as an Alberta cabinet minister and Peter Hyndman as a British Columbia cabinet minister. J.D. Hyndman died October 11, 1971 at the age of 97.

[See: Canadian Who's Who, 1936-37, 1967]

louis davies 'lou' hyndman, jr., q.c.

Born July 1, 1935, Edmonton, Alberta, son of Louis Davies Hyndman Sr., K.C. and Muriel MacKintosh. He was of English descent and an Anglican. His great-great-grandfather Benjamin Davies served as the Colonial Secretary of Prince Edward Island prior to Canadian Confederation in 1867. He returned as the Conservative member for the Queen's riding (P.E.I) in 1891 and served in federal cabinet from 1896 to 1901 when he was appointed as a Justice of the Supreme Court of Canada. 'Lou' Hyndman was educated at Edmonton where he attended the University of Alberta, graduating in Arts and subsequently in Law. He was admitted to the Alberta Bar in 1960 and practiced law with his father's legal firm of Field, Hyndman Field.

'Lou' Hyndman returned as the Progressive Conservative member for Edmonton Glenora in 1967. He was the executive assistant to the Minister of Citizenship and Immigration from 1962 to 1963. He became the Minister of Federal and Intergovernmental Affairs and Government House Leader in 1975. Four years later he became the Provincial Treasurer holding this portfolio for seven years. In 1986 he did not seek re-election and retired from politics at the age of 50. Later he served as Chancellor of the University of Alberta in the 1990s.

[See: Canadian Who's Who, 1990]

i

john irwin

Born October 10, 1869 at Picton, Ontario, son of Henry Irwin and Mary Charlton. He was of English descent and an Anglican. He settled in Alberta where he became a prominent Calgary grocer.

John Irwin returned as a Conservative member for the multi-member Calgary constituency in 1926. He sat in the Legislature as an opposition member for 14 years. In 1940 he did not seek re-election, but rather retired from politics at the age of 70, and later moved to British Columbia.

[See: Canadian Parliamentary Guide, 1940]

william carlos ives

Born October 30, 1873 at Compton, PQ, son of George Canning Ives (q.v), a member of the Northwest Mounted Police and later a prominent Pincher Creek rancher, and his wife Sara Abbie. His uncle was William Bullock Ives, Q.C. who served as member of the House Commons in the 1890s. He was of English descent and an Anglican. As a child, he attended a one-room school with his sister near his father's foothills ranch. Educated in Quebec, he attended McGill University and graduated in Law. He was admitted to the Northwest Territories Bar in 1901 and practiced law in Lethbridge in the legal firm of Conybeare and Walsh. He was an unsuccessful provincial candidate in 1905 and again in 1909.

W. Carlos Ives was appointed by Justice Minister C.J. Doherty as a Justice of the Alberta Supreme Court in 1914. In 1921 when the courts were re-organized, he was transferred to the Alberta Supreme Court: Trial Division. In 1935 he became the Chief Justice of the Trial Division. He retired from the Bench in 1944. Justice Ives was known as the 'cowboy judge'. In 1906 he had married Millicent May Troull of Woodstock, Ontario. They had one daughter, Elizabeth, who married Michael Burns, the only son of Senator Patrick 'the cattle king' Burns. W. Carlos Ives died July 10, 1950 at Calgary at the age of 77.

[See: Canadian Who's Who, 1936-37]

j

john ainslie jackson

Born March 25, 1875 at Egmondville, Ontario, son of George E. Jackson and his wife Elspeth Waugh. An uncle, Captain Thomas Jackson, had been one of the original Northwest Mounted Police in 1874. He was of Anglo-Irish descent and an Anglican. Educated at Seaforth, he attended the University Toronto where he qualified as a lawyer. He settled in Ponoka in 1903 where he practiced law. He was an unsuccessful provincial candidate in 1905 and again in 1909.

In 1913 J.A. Jackson was appointed by Justice Minister C.J. Doherty as Judge of the Lethbridge District Court. He served on the Bench for the next 32 years. Judge Jackson retired in 1945 and died on October 1, 1945 at Lethbridge at the age of 71.

[See: Alberta Past and Preset, 1924]

frederick charles jamieson, k.c.

Born May 18, 1875 in Carleton County, Ontario, son of James Jamieson Mary Ann Craig. He was of English-Ulster-Scottish descent and an Anglican. Educated at Kemptville, he then qualified as a teacher and taught in rural Ontario for two years. In 1895 he came to the Northwest Territories where he homesteaded near Lacombe. Later he moved to Strathcona and became a law articling student with A.C. Rutherford. He was admitted to the Northwest Territories Bar in 1899 and practiced law in the firm of Rutherford Jamieson. Jamieson volunteered for military service and saw active service with the Canadian Mounted Rifles in the South African War. After the war he returned to Strathcona continuing as a prominent Edmonton lawyer for the next 70 years. During WWI he went to Europe with the Canadian Expeditionary Force. He saw active service as the Commander of the First Canadian Division Mounted Troopers. After the war he again returned to his Edmonton legal practice.

Colonel F.C. Jamieson returned as Conservative member for Edmonton in the 1931 by-election. He sat in the Legislature for five years in opposition. In 1935 he was defeated in his re-election bid and retired from politics at the age of 60. He died October 4, 1966.

[See: Canadian Who's Who, 1964]

norman jaques

Born June 29, 1880 at London, England, son of Henry A. Jaques and his wife Mary Augusta Burrow. He was of French Huguenot descent and an Anglican. He was educated at Eastbourne College. He came to Canada as a young man in 1901 and homesteaded in the Mirror district. He became a well-known farmer in the area.

Norman Jacques returned as the Social Credit member for the Wetaskiwin riding in 1935. He sat in the House of Commons as a vocal opposition member until his death in January 1949.

[See: Canadian Who's Who, 1936-37]

william g. johnston

Born January 23, 1873 at Owen Sound, Ontario, son of James A. Johnston and his wife Helen A. Clark. He was of Scottish descent and an Anglican. He worked as a locomotive engineer for the Canadian Pacific Railway, based at Medicine Hat.

William Johnston returned as a Labour member for two-member Medicine Hat constituency in 1921. He sat in the Legislature as a UFA government supporter for four years. He died while still an incumbent at 1925.

halvar de la chyse jonson

Born April 14, 1941 at Athabasca, son of Huram Jonson and his wife Frances Christine. He was of Scandinavian descent and an Anglican. Educated at Boyle, he attended the University of Alberta, graduating in Education in 1963. He became a school teacher at Bentley and Ponoka, later returning to university for a graduate diploma in educational administration in 1976 and finally a Master's degree. He was appointed as Principal of Ponoka Composite High School.

Halvar Johnson returned as the Progressive Conservative member for Ponoka in 1982. He was re-elected in 1986, 1989, 1993, and 1997. He served as Minister of Education from 1992 to 1996, and was appointed as Minister of Health in 1997.

[See: Canadian Parliamentary Guide, 1997]

k

john henry william shore kemmis

Born July 18, 1867 near Madras, Southern India, son of Captain John G. Kemmis and his wife May Needham. His father was an officer in the Indian army. He was of English-Anglo-Irish descent and an Anglican. He was educated in Ireland. He came to Canada as a young man in 1893 and attended the Ontario Agricultural College at Guelph, Ontario. On the outbreak of the Northwest Rebellion in the spring of 1885, he enlisted with the Moose Mountain Scouts militia unit in Winnipeg and served as a dispatch rider between Calgary and Edmonton through hostile territory. After being demobilized at Regina, he homesteaded in the Fort District near Pincher Creek where he became a prominent rancher.

In 1898 he married Maude Elton who had been born at Lucknow, India. She was the daughter of a neighboring teacher rancher, Colonel B.W. Elton, a former British army officer. The young couple was married in the same church as his parents, Trinity Church, Bath, Somerset England. They returned to Canada to establish their home. John Kemmis was an unsuccessful provincial candidate in the 1905 election. John H.W.S. Kemmis returned as the Conservative member in the 1911 Pincher Creek by-election and sat in the Legislature for ten years as the spokesman for cattle ranchers' interests of southern Alberta. In 1921 he did not seek re-election and retired to his ranch. He moved to Calgary in 1924 and died October 13, 1942 at Calgary at the age of 75.

[See: Calgary Herald, April 24, 1939 and October 14, 1942]

stanley chandon stavely kerr, k.c.

Born April 6, 1889 at Toronto, son of senator James Kirkpatrick Kerr, K.C. and his second wife Adelaide Cecil Stanley-Pinhorne, niece of A. Stanley Hill, K.C. He was of Scottish descent and an Anglican. Educated at Upper Canada College, he attended the University of Toronto and then Osgoode Hall Law School. He also attended the Royal Staff College at Camberly, England He was admitted to the Ontario Bar in 1914 and the Alberta Bar in 1920. During WWI he saw active service as a major with the Royal Horse Guards on the Western Front. After the war he settled in Edmonton where he practiced law. He became a K.C. in 1936.

S.C.S. Kerr was appointed as judge of the Northern Alberta District Court in 1947. Two years later he was named Chief Judge of the Court. He died May 19, 1853 at Edmonton at the age of 65.

[See: Canadian Who's Who, 1936-1947]

w. j. cameron kirby

Born January 12, 1909 at Calgary, son of William J. Kirby who served for 50 years as the Rocky Mountain House postmaster, and his wife Catherine Georgine Gray. He was of English-Scottish-Irish descent and an Anglican. His grandfather, Joseph Kirby, fought in the American Civil War of 1861-165. He was educated at Hanna. During WWII he enlisted in the Canadian Army and saw active service as a Captain in the artillery of the Pacific. After the war he attended the University of British Columbia and the Vancouver Law School. He was admitted to the Alberta Bar and practiced law in Red Deer. W.J. Cameron Kirby returned as the Progressive Conservative member for Red Deer in the by-election of February 15, 1954. He sat in the Legislature for five years in opposition. In August 1958, he was named the Alberta Progressive Conservative leader and held this position for two years. In 1959 he was defeated by Social Creditor William K. Ure. In 1960 he was appointed as a District Judge and was later transferred to the Alberta Court of Queen's bench. Mr. Justice Kirby retired from the bench on January 12, 1984.

[See: Canadian Who's Who, 1984]

1

dr. john drought lauder

Born in January of 1857 in County Meath, Ireland. He was an Anglican of Anglo-Irish descent. He attended Trinity College, Dublin before going to Liverpool, England to study medicine. He came to Canada in 1975 and became an assistant to Dr. Kerr in Nova Scotia. In 1876 Dr. Lauder enlisted in the Northwest Mounted police and served at Winnipeg, Fort Pelly and finally Fort Calgary. After leaving the force, he worked as a cowboy on the Cochrane Ranch. On the outbreak of the Northwest Rebellion in 1885, he enlisted as an officer with the Alberta Rifles militia under Major Hatton. After being demobilized, he became a Calgary rancher.

John D. Lauder returned as one of the two elected members for Calgary in the N.W.T. Executive Council. He served on council for two years. In 1892 he became an Innisfail physician.

[See: History of Alberta, Vol. 2, 1912]

clarence merbin leitech, q.c.

Born January 13, 1926 at Creelman, Saskatchwan, son of Peter Howard Leitch and his wife Martha Walter. He was of English descent and an Anglican. Educated in rural schools, he served in the Royal Canadian Navy in WWII. After the war he attended the University of Alberta, graduating in Law in 1952 and was admitted to the Alberta Bar in 1953. He served as a member of the Calgary Police Commission in the late 1960s.

C. 'Merv' Leitch returned as the Progressive Conservative member for Calgary Egmont in 1971 and sat in the Legislature for 11 years. He served in Premier Lougheed's cabinet, first as the Attorney General from 1971 to 1975, then as Provincial Treasurer from 1975 to 1979, and finally as Minister of Energy and Natural resources from 1979 to 1982. He was recognized as one of the premier's closest friends and one of the most effective members of Lougheed's cabinet. In 1983, he did not seek re-elections, retired from politics and retired to his private law practice in Calgary. He died June 30, 1990 at Calgary.

[See: Canadian Who's Who, 1979; Canadian Parliamentary Guide, 1908)

william g. lesick

Born June 10, 193 at Spedden, Alberta, son of William Alexander Lesick and his wife Emily Syrotuk. He was of Ukrainian descent and an Anglican. Educated at Andrew, he attended the University of Alberta where he graduated in Pharmacy and practiced his profession in Edmonton. He served in the Canadian army during WWII.

William Lesick returned as the Progressive Conservative member for Edmonton East in 1984. He served in the House of Commons for four years. In 1988 he was defeated by New Democrat Ross Harvey and then retired from politics at the age of 65. In 1998 he was residing in retirement at Edmonton.

[See: Canadian Parliamentary Guide, 1985]

106 edgar peter **lougheed**, o.c., q.c.

Born July 24, 1928 at Calgary, son of Edgar Donald Lougheed and his wife Erna Bauld. He was of Anglo-Irish descent and an Anglican. He was the grandson of Senator J.A. Lougheed (q.v.). His ancestors played a significant part in the development of what is called Rupert's Land since 1817. His great-great-grandfather Richard Hardisty (1790-1865) was born in the London parish of St. Martins-in-the-Field. As a young man he saw active service as a British army officer in the Peninsular War and the battle of Waterloo in June 1815. He later became an employee of the Hudson's Bay Company fur trading company rising to the position of Chief Factor. Another of his ancestors was married to Lord Strathcona. Educated at Calgary, Peter Lougheed attended the University of Alberta, graduating in Arts and then in Law. During his student days at the University of Alberta he played for the Edmonton Eskimo Football team. In 1952 he married Jeanne Estelle Rogers, daughter of Dr. Lawrence Rogers of Camrose. Later he attended Harvard University where he earned an M.B.A. in 1954. He was admitted to the Alberta Bar in the same year and practiced law in Calgary. In February 1965 he was chosen as leader of the Alberta Progressive Conservative party, succeeding A. Milton Harradance (later Mr. Justice Harradance).

E. Peter Lougheed returned as the Progressive Conservative member for Calgary West in 1967 and sat in the Legislature for 18 years. He led his party to victory in the August 1971 provincial election. A total of 49 Progressive Conservatives returned as compared to 25 Social Creditors and one New Democrat. He served as Premier of the province for 14 years. In late 1985 he resigned the premiership, did not seek re-election in the 1986 election, and retired from politics at the age of 57. In 1998 he was residing in Calgary.

[See: Canadian Who's Who, 1964-66]

james alexander lougheed, q.c.

Born September 1, 1854 at Brampton, Upper Canada, son of John Lougheed and his wife Mary Ann Alexander. Educated at Toronto and called to the Bar of Ontario in 1877. In 1883 he settled at Calgary where he as called to the Bar of the Northwest Territories. In 1884 he married Isabella 'Belle' Hardisty, daughter of William Hardisty, Chief Factor of the Hudson's Bay Company and grand-daughter of Richard Hardisty (q.v), also a factor of the Hudson's Bay Company.

James Alexander Lougheed was named as Alberta's second Senator in 1889 by Prime Minister John A. Macdonald. He sat in the upper chamber for 37 years. In 1906 he became the Conservative leader of the Senate Opposition. Five years later when Robert Borden became Prime Minister, Lougheed was named to the cabinet as Minister without Portfolio and government leader in the Senate. In 1920 Prime Minister Arthur Meighen appointed Senator Lougheed as Minister of the Interior, and he held this portfolio until the Conservatives were voted out of office in December 1921. He died in November 3, 1925 at Ottawa at the age of 71. His funeral, half at Calgary's Holy Redeemer Cathedral, was one of the largest in the city's history. His grandson is E. Peter Lougheed (q.v.)

[See: Canadian Who's Who, 1912; Macmillan Dictionary of Biography, 1978]

eric lowther

Born August 31, 1954. He was an Anglican. He attended the University of Alberta, graduating with a science degree in 1977. He worked in the Alberta telecommunications industry as an account and distribution manager for AGT and then for Telus. He was active in community service organizations serving on the boards of a number of child-oriented associations and the Y.M.C.A.

Eric Lowther returned as the Reform member for the Calgary-Centre riding in the 1997 federal election. He was appointed as deputy critic for Industry in 1997.

[See: Canadian Parliamentary Guide, 1997]

william thomas lucas

Born July 26, 1875 at Bailieboro, Ontario. He was of Irish descent and an Anglican. Educated at Bailieboro, he attended the Shaw Business School at Toronto and the Ontario Agricultural College at Guelph. He came to Alberta as a young man and homesteaded in the Lougheed district where he became an active member of the United Farmers of Alberta movement.

William T. Lucas returned as the UFA-Progressive member for the Camrose riding in 1921. He sat in the House of Commons as an opposition member for 14 years. After 1925 he represented the Camrose riding. In 1935 he was defeated in his re-election bid by the Social Credit candidate, J.A. Marshall, and retired from politics at the age of 60.

[See: Canadian Who's Who, 1936-37]

frank c. lynch-staunton

Born March 8, 1905 at Pincher Creek, son of Richard Lynch-Staunton and his wife Isabel March Wilson. He became an Anglican later in life. Educated at Pincher Creek, he attended Western Canada College, Calgary and the University of Alberta where he graduated in Engineering in 1927. He worked in the oil industry for two years before going into partnership with his father on the family ranch in 1929. He served in the Militia and Army reserved with the rank of major from 1934 to 1942. Active in civic politics, he served as a municipal councilor of the district of Pincher Creek. He was also on the Senate of the University of Lethbridge.

Frank C. Lynch-Staunton was sworn in as the eleventh Lieutenant Governor of Alberta in October 1979. In 1983 he was married (he had been a widower since 1979) to Muriel Shaw, a longtime neighbor and friend, in All Saints Anglican Cathedral, Edmonton thereby becoming an Anglican. He served as Lieutenant Governor until 1985 and died in September 1990. His funeral was held at Cowley Anglican Church in Southern Alberta and a memorial service at Christ Church, Edmonton which had been his parish church during his time of residence in Edmonton.

[See: Canadian Parliamentary Guide, 1980; File, Legislature Library] m

112 roberta catherine **macadam** [mrs. price]

Born June 21, 1881 at Sarnia, Ontario, daughter Robert MacAdam, a newspaper publisher, and his wife Catherine Born. She was an Anglican of Anglo-Irish descent on her paternal side. Educated at Guelph, she attended Chicago University. As a young woman, she came to Alberta and settled at Edmonton where she was in charge of 'the domestic science' department of the government. She also helped in the establishment of Women's Institutes across rural Alberta. At the outbreak of WWI, Miss MacAdam enlisted in the nursing corps. She received a commission and went overseas with the Canadian Expeditionary Force. Lt. MacAdam served in the United Kingdom.

In the Special Overseas Soldier legislative election to send two service personnel to the Legislature, Lt. MacAdam and Padre Captain (Methodist) Robert Pearson returned. Initially she sat as Miss MacAdam, but on September 21, 1920 she married her brother's law partner, Harvey Stinson Price, of Calgary. In 1921 she did not seek re-election and retired from provincial politics. The Prices homesteaded for a decade in the Peace River Country before finally settling in Calgary. She was one of the five Alberta women who in 1929 persuaded the British Privy Council that women were persons under the law and could be summoned to sit in the Canadian Senate.

[See: Canadian Parliamentary Guide, 1921]

maitland stewart mccarthy

Born February 15, 1972 at Orangeville, Ontario, son of Judge Bolton McCarthy and his wife Frances Stewart. He was of Anglo-Irish descent and an Anglican. Educated at Port hope, he attended the University of Toronto, graduating in Arts and then Law. He was admitted to the Ontario Bar in 1897 and practiced law in Loughton County. In 1900 he married Eva Florence Watson of Hamilton. They moved to Alberta in 1903 and settled in Calgary where he practiced law.

M.S. McCarthy returned as the Conservative member for the Calgary riding in 1904 and sat in the House of Commons as an opposition member for seven years. In 1911 he did not seek re-election. Justice Minister C.J. Doherty appointed M.S. McCarthy as a Justice of the Alberta Supreme Court in 1914. When the courts were reorganized in 1921 he was transferred to the Alberta Supreme Court: Trial Division. He retired from the Bench in 1926 and died May 27, 1930 at Montreal at the age of 58.

[See: Canadian Who's Who, 1912]

george mcclellan

Born in 1908 at Moose Jaw Saskatchewan. He was an Anglican. He enlisted in the R.C.M.P. in 1932 and rose through the ranks becoming commissioner in 1963 and retiring from the force in 1967. In 1967 he was appointed as Alberta's first ombudsman and first provincial ombudsman in Canada. He defined the main focus of his position as the improvement of provincial government administrative practices so as to minimize future repetition of injustices. Following his retirement from the post in 1974 he was appointed by Premier Lougheed as Chairman of the Alberta Rent Regulation Appeal Board. He was awarded honorary Doctor of Laws degrees by both the Royal Military College (1976) and the University of Alberta (1978). He died July 19 1982 at Edmonton.

[See: Provincial Government Profile, Legislative Library, Edmonton]

peter l.p. macdonnell, m.c,. q.c.

Born in 1919. He attended Queen's University, graduating in Arts and Cambridge University, graduating in Arts by the Inns of Court (England). He was admitted to the English Bar and the Ontario Bar in 1947. He came to Alberta in 1950 where he was admitted to the Alberta Brand practiced law in Edmonton with the legal firm of Milner, Steer. He created a Queen's Counsel in 1963.

Peter L.P. Macdonnell served as the Chancellor of the Anglican Archdiocese of Edmonton from 1972 to 1985. In the 1984 Canadian Law List, Macdonnell is listed as the senior partner in the Edmonton legal firm of Milner, Steer.

dr. harold wigmore mcgill

Born December 21, 1879 at Norwood, Ontario, son of Edward McGill and his wife Henrietta Wigmore. He was of Anglo-Irish descent and an Anglican. He attended the University of Manitoba, Winnipeg, where he graduated in medicine. He settled and practiced medicine in Calgary. He was active in civic politics, serving as an alderman from 1927 to 1930. During WWI he served as a surgeon with the Canadian Expeditionary Force and the 5th Canadian Field Ambulance.

Dr. Harold McGill returned as a Conservative member of the multi-Calgary constituency in 1930. He sat in the Legislature for three years as a member of opposition. In 1933 he vacated his seat to enter the federal civil service. He was appointed as Deputy Superintendent General for Indian Affairs for all of Canada.

[See: Canadian Who's Who, 1938]

gordon thomas w. miniely

Born October 25, 1939 at Bonnyville, son of Gorden Miniely and his wife Irene Hazel. He was an Anglican.

Gordon T.W. Miniely returned as the Progressive Conservative member for Edmonton Entre in 1971 and sat in the Legislature for eight years. Premier Lougheed appointed him Provincial Treasurer in his first cabinet. In 1975 he was transferred to the Hospitals and Medical Care portfolio. He retired from politics in 1979. In 1998 he was the senior partner in the Miniely and Towers firm of chartered accountants in Edmonton.

[See: Canadian Who's Who, 1979]

archibald percy mitchell

Born April 13, 1880 at New Cross, Kent, England, son of Walter Mitchell, and auctioneer, and his wife Kate Fitch. He was of English descent and an Anglican. Educated at Christ Church school, Brighton, he came to Alberta as a young man in 1903, homesteaded near Millet and also became an auctioneer. He was recognized as an expert on antiques. Active in community affairs and civic politics he was on the school board for six years and served as mayor of Millet for seven years.

Archibald P. Mitchell returned as the Liberal member for Leduc in 1930 and sat in the legislature as an opposition member for five years. In 1935 he was defeated by Socred R. Earl Ansley and retired from politics at the age of 55. In 1945 he retired and moved to British Columbia where he died January 22, 1968 at Victoria at the age of 88.

[See: Canadian Parliamentary Guide, 1935]

arnold fraser moir, q.c.

Born in 1918 at Fort Macleod, Alberta, son of Harold C. Moir and his wife Florence who had been born at Old Chelsea, Quebec. His father was a Milk River merchant who had been an unsuccessful Warner candidate in 1935. He was of Scottish descent and an Anglican. Educated at Milk River, he attended the University of Alberta, graduating in Arts 1942 and then in Law in 1946. He was awarded the Chie Justice Gold Medal and a Viscount Bennett Scholarship. He attended Harvard University, graduating with a Masters in Law degree in 1948. Returning to Edmonton, he articled with Ronald Martland of the Milner, Steer legal firm prior to being admitted to the Alberta Bar in 1948. He practiced law in Calgary with the firm Wood, Buchanan and created a Queen's Counsel in 1960.

Justice Minister Otto Lang appointed Arnold F. Moir as a Justice of the Alberta Supreme Court: Appellate Division in 1973. When the courts were reorganized in 1979 he was transferred to the newly created Alberta Court of Appeal. He served as the Chancellor of the Anglican Archdiocese of Edmonton from 1985 to 1988. He died September 24, 1988 at Edmonton.

[See: Alberta Judicial Biographical Dictionary, 1990]

n

carl olof nickle

Born July 12, 1914 at Winnipeg, Manitoba, son of Samuel A. Nickle and his wife Olga Simonson. His father was of Anglo-Irish descent and had come to the United States in 1942. His mother was of Swedish descent. He was Anglican. Educated at Calgary, he attended Mount Royal College. He worked at Calgary radio station CFCN in 1936. On the development of oil in the Turner Valley he founded his own publication, The Daily Oil Bulletin, in 1937. He served with the Calgary Highlanders Militia from 1930 to 1949 and he sat active service as an officer with the Calgary Highlanders in the Italian campaign of 1943-45.

Carl Olof Nickle returned as the Progressive Conservative member for Clary East in the 1951 by-election. He sat in the House of Commons as an opposition member for six years. In 1957 he did not seek re-election, retiring from politics at the age of 43. He died in 1992 at Calgary.

[See: Canadian Who's Who, 1973]

walter grant notley

Born January 19, 1939 at Didsbury, son of James Walter Notley and his wife Frances Mary Grant. He was of English descent and an Anglican. Educated at Olds, he attended the University of Alberta, graduating in Arts. He became a New Democratic party official and was chosen as the Alberta New Democratic leader in 1968. He was an unsuccessful provincial candidate in 1963, 1967 and again in a 1969 by-election.

Grant Notley returned as the New Democratic member for Spirit River-Fairview in 1971. He sat in the Legislature for 12 years as a vocal critic of the Lougheed administration. On October 19, 1984 he was killed in a plane crash.

[See: Canadian Parliamentary Guide, 1983]

o

124   charles gerald o'connor, k.c.

Born December 3, 1890 at Walkerton, Ontario, son of Frederick Sheppard O'Connor and Maria Isabella Hamilton. He was an Anglican of Anglo-Irish descent. [His elder brothers, George Bligh O'Connor (q.v.) became Chief Justice of Alberta.] Educated at Edmonton, he attended Alberta College. He then studied law in Toronto's Osgoode Hall, read law with Griesbach and O'Connor in 1912 and 1913 and was admitted to the Alberta Bar in 1914. During WWI he enlisted in the army and went overseas as an officer with Canadian Expeditionary Force. He saw active service with the machine gun corps on the Western Front. After the war he returned to Edmonton where he joined the prominent legal firm of Griesbach O'Connor and O'Connor. Active in civic politics, he served as an alderman in 1932 and 1933. He was also a president of the Edmonton Chamber of Commerce.

C. Gerald O'Connor returned as the Liberal member for the multi-member Edmonton constituency in 1935. He sat in the Legislature as an opposition member. In 1940 he was narrowly defeated at the polls and retired from politics to return to the legal profession. He had created a King's Counsel in 1939 and in 1945 and was appointed a Judge of the Federal Exchequer Court. He died November 16, 1949 at Ottawa.

[See: Canadian Who's Who, 1948]

george bligh o'connor, k.c.

The elder brother of Charles Gerald O'Connor (q.v.), he was born March 16, 1883 at Walkerton, Ontario. He was an Anglican. Educated at Walkerton, he later attended Toronto's Osgoode Hall law school. He was admitted to the Ontario Bar in 1905. He settled in Edmonton where he was admitted to the Northwest Territories Bar, also in 1905. He practiced law with the firm Griesbach O'Connor and O'Connor which was the most prominent legal firm in western Canada for 40 some years. Griesbach became a senator while the two O'Connors became judges. He created a King's Counsel in 1913 and the same year married Hannah Margaret Fairlie, daughter of the Reverend John Fairlie.

George Bligh O'Connor was appointed to the Alberta Supreme Court: Trial Division in 1940 and elevated to the Alberta Supreme Court: Appellate Division in 1945. On the death of 86 year-old Horace Harvey (q.v.) in 1949, Mr. Justice G.B. O'Connor became the Chief Justice of Alberta. He died while still on the Bench in January 1957.

[See: Canadian Who's Who, 1952]

p

mary irene parlby (née marryat)

Born January 9, 1868 at London, England, daughter of Colonel Ernest Lindsay Marryat who served in the Royal Engineers and his wife Elizabeth Lynch, daughter of General Patrick Lynch of Ballinrobe, County Mayo, Ireland, She was of English/Anglo-Irish descent and an Anglican. Her grandfather, S. Marryat was the M.P. for Wembley who voted against the Reform Bill in 1832, while her great uncle was the novelist Frederick Marryat (1792-1848) who wrote Mr. Midshipman Easy, and Children of the New Forest. Mary Irene was educated privately and spent part of her childhood in India, where her father was on active service. In 1896, she came to Canada on a visit. While at Alix, north of Red Deer, she met and married Walter H. Parlby, son of the Reverend John Hall Parlby who was a homesteader in the area. Mrs. Parlby became active in the Women's Branch of the United Farmers of Alberta and by 1918 she was on the UFA executive.

Mrs. M. Irene Parlby returned as the UFA member for Ponoka in 1921 and sat in the Legislature for 14 years as a Minister Without Portfolio. In 1935 she did not seek re-election and retired from politics.

[See: Canadian Who's Who, 1960-61]

robert patterson

Born April 11, 1855 in County Tipperary, Ireland, son of George Patterson and his wife Mary. He was an Anglican of Anglican-Irish descent. He was a cousin of Judge Wright. Educated at Kilkenny, at the age of 21 he came to Canada and enlisted in the Northwest Mount Police. He served at Fort Macleod until 1880 where he left the force and became a cattle and horse rancher near Fort Macleod. He built the first brick residence in the community.

Robert Patterson returned as the Conservative member for Macleod in the October 1910 by-election. He sat in the Legislature as an opposition member for seven years. In 1917 he was defeated in his re-election bid by Geore Skelding, a coal merchant. He then retired from politics at the age of 62. He died in 1938.

[See: Canadian Who's Who, 1913]

frederick h. peacock

Born November 23, 1916 at Calgary, son of James Peacock and his wife Ellen Johnstone. He was of English descent and an Anglican. Educated at Calgary, he attended the University of California. During WWII he enlisted in the Royal Canadian Air Force and served as a squadron leader in northwest Europe. After the war he became a prominent Calgary businessman.

Frederick H. Peacock returned as the Progressive Conservative member for Calgary Currie in 1971 and sat in the Legislature for eight years. In 1975 Premier Lougheed appointed him as Minister of Industry and Commerce and he held the portfolio for four years. In 1979 Peacock did not seek re-election, retiring from politics. He continued his public service, however, following his appointment as Alberta Horse Racing Commissioner.

[See: Canadian Parliamentary Guide, 1975]

charles stuart pingle

Born October 16, 1880 at Morris, Manitoba, son of Warren Hume Pingle and his wife Georgina. He was an Anglican of English descent. He came to the Northwest Territories as a young man and became a well-known pharmacist and businessman in Medicine Hat. During WWI he enlisted and went overseas as an officer with the Canadian Expeditionary Force. Captain Pingle saw active service on the Western Front.

Charles Pingle returned as the Liberal member for Redcliff in 1913 and sat in the Legislature for a total of 12 years. From 1918 to 1925 he served as Speaker. In 1921 he lost his seat, but was re-elected to the chamber in the 1925 Medicine Hat by-election. He died in as an incumbent in 1928.

[See: Canadian Parliamentary Guide, 1928]

david clifford prowse

Born March 20, 2910 at Taber, Alberta, son of James Harper Prowse and his wife Elizabeth Short Colquhoun. His father was a Taber lawyer who had come to Alberta from Prince Edward Island in 1910. He was of Scottish descent and an Anglican. Educated at Taber, he attended the University of Alberta. On the outbreak of WWII, he enlisted in the Royal Canadian Air Force and saw active service as a bomber pilot in northwest Europe. In 1943 his plane was shot down over Germany and he became a prisoner of war. He lost a hip as a result of the plane crash. After the war, he returned to university, graduating in Commerce and then Law; he was admitted to the Alberta Bar in 1951. He practiced law in Calgary as a member of the legal firm of Fenerty, Fenetry, McGillivray, Robertson, Prowse and Brennan. D. Clifford Prowse was appointed as a Justice of the Alberta Supreme Court: Appellate Division by Justice Minister Otto Land in 1972. When the courts were reorganized in 1979 he was transferred to the newly created Alberta Court of Appeal. He died August 1988 at Calgary.

hubert s. prowse, q.c.

Born December 8, 1922 at Taber Alberta, the youngest son of James Harper Prowse, Sr. and his wife Elizabeth Short Colquhoun. He was of Scottish descent and an Anglican. His ancestors came from Prince Edward Island and were active Conservatives; two had served in the Senate. His elder brothers were Senator J. Harper Prowse (q.v.) and Justice D. Clifford Prowse (q.v.) of the Alberta Court of Appeal. He was educated at Taber. During WWII he enlisted in the Canadian army and saw active service in the Italian campaign. After the war he attended the University of Alberta, graduating in Commerce and then Law. He articled with his father, was admitted to the Alberta Bar in 1951 and practiced in Lethbridge. He was created a Queen's Counsel in 1968 and then moved to Calgary where he joined the legal firm of Fenerty, Robertson and Prowse.

j. harper prowse, q.c.

Born July 2, 1913 at Taber, Alberta, son of James H. Prowse, a Taber lawyer, and his wife Elizabeth Short Colquhoun. He was of ethnic Scottish descent and an Anglican. Educated at Mifford, he attended the Edmonton Normal School. Later he attended the University of Alberta, graduating in Arts. He then became an Edmonton newspaper reporter. During WWII he enlisted in the Canadian Army and saw active service in the Italian campaign in 1944. He was seriously wounded.

In January 1945 he was elected to represent the army in the Alberta legislature. He sat in the Chamber for 14 years. In 1947 he was chosen as the Alberta Liberal leader. He held this position for 11 years. While a member, he attended the University of Alberta graduating in Law. He was admitted to the Alberta Bar in 1958. In 1959 he did no seek re-election. He was an unsuccessful federal candidate in 1962 and 1963. Prowse was summoned to the senate in 1966 where he sat for ten years. He died in 1976.

[See: Canadian Parliamentary Guide, 1975]

q

victor quelch, m.c.

Born December 13, 1891 at Georgetown, British Guyana, son of John J. Quelch and his wife Gertrude Saintsbury. He was of ethnic English descent and an Anglican. Educated at Leeds, England, he came to Alberta in 1909. During WWII he saw active service as a captain in the 14th Canadian Battalion. In September 1918 he was awarded the Military Cross for Bravery. After the war he returned to his Morrin farm.

Victor Quelch returned as the Social Credit member for the Acadia riding in 1935. He sat in the House of Commons for 22 years. In 1958 he did not seek re-election and retired from politics at the age of 67.

[See: Canadian Who's Who, 1955]

r

daniel lee redman

Born October 4, 1889 at Oil City, Ontario, son of D.B. Redmun and his wife A.M. Wilson. He was of English/Scottish descent and an Anglican. Educated at Petrolia High School, he attended King's College, London and the Inns of Court, London. He received his LLB from the University of Manitoba. He practiced law at Calgary as a member of the Lougheed, Bennett, McLean law firm. He was a prominent Calgary figure serving on numerous board of directors. During WWI he was a Captain in the 103rd Regiment Calgary Rifles and enlisted in the Canadian Expeditionary Force in 1914. He was wounded in 1915.

Daniel Lee Redman returned as a Unionist pro-government member for Calgary East in the general election of 1917. He served in the House of Commons for four years as a private member. In 1921 he did not seek re-election and retired from politics at the age of 32.

[See: Canadian Parliamentary Guide, 1918]

ezra hounfield riley

Born in June 1866 at Toronto, eldest son of Thomas B. Riley, a Calgary pioneer settler and his wife Georgiana Jane Hounfield. He was of English descent and an Anglican. He took over the family Nose Hill ranch.

Ezra H. Riley returned as the Liberal member for Gleichen in the 1906 by-election. He sat in the Legislature for four years. In 1910 he resigned his seat in protest against the way in which the successor premier Rutherford was chosen. Prime Minister Laurier, Frank Oliver (MP for Edmonton) and the Lieutenant Governor of Alberta had arranged among themselves that Arthur Sifton would become Rutherford's successor – all without consulting the Liberal legislative caucus. Ezra H. Riley failed in his re-election attempt in the resulting by-election.

[See: Canadian Parliamentary Guide, 1911]

[Note: no relation to Senator Daniel E. Riley (1860-1948) who was also a Calgary rancher]

harold william hounfield riley

Born December 15, 1877 at Montreal, son of Thomas B. Riley and Georgiana Jane Hounfield and brother of Ezra Hounfield Riley (q.v.). He was of English descent and a prominent Anglican. He came to the Northwest Territories with his family and became a Calgary investment dealer. From 1905 to 1910 he served as the deputy provincial secretary and also as a Calgary alderman.

Harold Riley returned as the Conservative member for Gleichen in the October 31, 1911 by-election, defeated his brother who had previously resigned his Liberal seat. He sat in the Legislature for two years and was defeated in the 1913 general election by Liberal P.J. McArthur. He died in 1946.

[See: Canadian Parliamentary Guide, 1912]

harold william riley, q.c.

Born January 1, 1903 at Calgary, son of H.W.H Riley (q.v.) and his wife Alpha Maud Keen. He was of English descent and an Anglican. Educated at Calgary he attended the University of Alberta, graduating in Law in 126. He was admitted to the Alberta Bar in 1927 and was a prominent Calgary lawyer for the next 30 years. He was a senior partner in the legal firm of Macleod Riley McDermid. He created a Q.C. Riley was an unsuccessful Liberal candidate for the Calgary West riding in 1953.

Justice Minister Stuart Garson appointed Harold W. Riley as a Justice of the Alberta Supreme Court: Trial Division in 1956. He was recognized as being one of the ablest jurists in the province. In 1973 Justice H.W. Riley retired from the bench and died November 6, 1979 at Calgary.

[See: Canadian Parliamentary Guide, 1913]

robert melville roberts

Born December 15, 1879 at Pedee, Cedar County, Iowa, son of Scottish-born parents. He was an Anglican. He attended the State University of Iowa, graduating in Law, and practiced law in Iowa City. He came to Canada as a young man where he settled at High River establishing his law practice.

Robert Melville Roberts returned as the Liberal member for High River in 1909. He sat in the Legislature as a government back bencher for four years. In 1913 he did not seek re-election and retired from politics at the age of 33.

[See: Canadian Parliamentary Guide, 1913]

rev. william a. roberta

Born July 22, 1954 at Hamilton, Ontario, son of Edward W, Roberts and his wife Elsie Irene Lelsie. He was of English descent and an Anglican. He attended Trent University, graduating in Arts in 1976. He then attended Harvard University Divinity School (M. Div., 1979) and was ordained a priest. Later he was a Rockefellar Scholar at Princeton University. He came to Alberta where he became the vicar at All Saints Anglican Cathedral.

William Roberts returned as the New Democratic member for Edmonton Centre in 1986 and he sat in the Legislature for seven years acting as federal and Intergovernmental Affairs critic. In 1993 he did not seek re-election and retired from politics at the age of 49. Later he moved to Denver, Colorado.

[See: Canadian Parliamentary Guide, 1993]

charles w. robinson, o.b.e.

Born in 1975 in Yorkshire, England. He was of English descent and an Anglican. His family came to Canada in 1897 and homesteaded in the Northwest Territories. In 1900 he enlisted in the Northwest Mounted Police and transferred to Lord Strathcona Horse. He actively served in the South African War. After his military service he became a pioneer settler in the Munson district near Drumheller in Alberta where he established a homestead at Fox Creek. On the outbreak of WWI he re-enlisted in the Canadian army. He raised a battalion and saw active service at its colonel on the Western Front. In 1916 he was a victim of the first German gas attack at St. Julien and he was also seriously wounded. Col. Robinson was awarded the O.B.E. Colonel Charles W. Robinson was an unsuccessful candidate in 1935. He died in 1963 at Victoria.

neville sydney roper

Born March 5, 1922 at Camrose, son of Henry Basil Sydney Roper and his wife Amy Burchnal. He was of English descent and an Anglican. Educated at Rimbey, he became a local businessman. He served in the R.C.A.F. during WWII (1941-1946). Active in civic politics he served as a councilor in Rimbey from 1951 to 1961 and as mayor from 1961 to 1966. He was also chairman of the Battle River Planning Commission for three years. He was an unsuccessful candidate in 1963.

Neville S. Rope returned as the Social Credit member for Ponoka in 1967 and he sat in the Legislature as a government back bencher for one term. In 1971 he was defeated in his re-election bid by Tory Dr. D.J. McCrimmon. He then retired from politics at the age of 49.

[See: Canadian Parliamentary Guide, 1971]

S

henry p. otty savary, k.c.

Born in 1878 at Annapolis, Nova Scotia, son of Alfred William Savary (1831-1920) and his wife Bessie Crookshank, daughter of Henry P. Otty of St. John, New Brunswick. His father was a member of the first Canadian parliament and later served a judge. He was of English/German descent and an Anglican. His ancestors were among the first English settlers of Annapolis county. Educated in Annapolis, he attended King's College (University) where he qualified as a lawyer. He came to Alberta in 1909 and settled at Calgary where he became a prominent lawyer. He served as the Chancellor of the Anglican diocese of Calgary from 1923 until his death in 1929.

[Se: The Canadian Dictionary of Parliament 1867-1967, 1968]

stanley stanford schumacher

Born June 12, 1933 at Hanna, son of Louis Peter Schumacher and his wife Gladys Geraldine Knudson. He was of German/Norwegian descent and an Anglican. Educated at Drumheller and Calgary, he attended the University of British Columbia, graduating first in Commerce and then in Law. He was admitted to the Alberta Bar in 1960 and practiced law in Drumheller.

Stanley S. Schumacher returned as the Progressive Conservative member for the Palliser riding in 1968 and he sat in the House of Commons as an opposition member for 11 years. In 1979, he ran as an Independent after losing his party's nomination, in which he was defeated.

Turning to provincial politics, Schumacher returned as the Progressive Conservative member for Drumheller in 1986 and he sat in the Legislature for 12 years. Schumacher was the Speaker of the Alberta Legislature from 1993 to 1997. In the 1997 election, when his constituency disappeared as a result of redistribution of seats, he did not seek re-election and retired from politics. In 1998 he was practicing law at Drumheller.

[See: Canadian Who's Who, 1997]

david lynch scott, q.c.

Born August 21, 1845 at Brampton, Canada West. He was an Anglican. Educated at Brampton, he later studied law and was called to the Ontario Bar in 1870. He practiced law in Orangeville, Ontario and after 1882 in Regina, Northwest Territories. He created a Q.C. in 1885 and acted as counsel for the Crown at the trial of Louis Riel in 1885.

In 1894 David Scott was named to the Bench of the Northwest Territories and transferred in 1905 to the Bench of Alberta. In 1921 he became the Chief Justice of Alberta. He died at South Cooking Lake July 26, 1924.

[See: Macmillan Dictionary of Canadian Biography, 1978]

richard secord

Born July 19, 1860 at Burford, Canada West, son of James R. Secord and Jane Manly. He was of United Empire Loyalist stock and an Anglican. One of his ancestors was Laura Secord, heroine of the War of 1810. He was educated at Brantford, Ontario and came to the Northwest Territories as a young man. He settled at Edmonton where he became a prominent merchant.

Richard Secord returned as the member for Edmonton in 1902 and sat in the Northwest Territories Legislative Assembly for two years. He then vacated his seat and turned to federal politics. He was an unsuccessful Conservative candidate for the Edmonton riding in the 1904 general election as Liberal incumbent Frank Oliver retained the seat.

[See: Canadian Parliamentary Guide, 1903]

gary severtson

Born March 18, 1922 at Lethbridge. He was an Anglican. Educated at Innisfail, he became a farmer in the Innisfail area.

Gary Severtson returned as the Progressive Conservative member for Innisfail in 1989. He was re-elected in 1993 and 1997. He served on the vestry at St. John's Church, Innisfail for 15 years.

[See: Canadian Parliamentary Guide, 1997]

john w. shera

Born September 11, 1867 in County Rosscommon, Ireland, son of John Shera and his wife Jane Stevenson. He was of Anglo-Irish descent and Anglican. He came to Canada as a child with his family and was educated at Toronto. On the outbreak of the Northwest Rebellion in 1885, his father enlisted in a militia, saw active service in the campaign and was taken prisoner near Eagle Hills. Young John W. Shera finally settled at Fort Saskatchewan where he became a prominent merchant after working for the Edmonton firm of McDougall and Secord for several years. He also operated a sawmill and was a lumber merchant.

John W. Shera returned as a member for Victoria (N.W.T.) in 1898. He sat in the Territorial Legislative Assembly for seven years until the assembly ceased to exist. In 1905 he was an unsuccessful Conservative candidate for the Victoria constituency in the first Alberta general election. He then retired from politics at the age of 38. In 1912 he became the federal collector of customs at Edmonton. He retired in 1935. He died May 27, 1955 at Edmonton at the age of 86. J.W. Shera was the last survivor of the Northwest Territories Legislative Assembly.

[See: Alberta: Past and Present, 1924]

tom sigurdson

Born March 7, 1957 at Vancouver. B.C., son of George Sigurdson and his wife Eveline Lindsell. He was an Anglican. Educated at Vancouver College, he attended the University of British Columbia and the University of Victoria. He became active in the New Democratic Party serving as Executive Assistant to the party leader Grant Notley and Director and Membership and Finance for the Alberta N.D.P.

Tom Sigurdson returned as the N.D.P. member for Edmonton-Belmont in 1986. He sat in the Legislature for seven years, but was defeated in his 1993 re-election bid.

[See: Canadian Parliamentary Guide, 1989]

walter dever skrine

Born August 18, 1863 at the ancestral family home at Warleigh Lodge, Wimbledon, Surrey, England, son of the Reverend Claremont William Skrine, Anglican vicar of Emmanuel Church and his wife Mary Ann Benne. He was of English descent and an Anglican. His ancestors held lands from Bath Abbey, Somerset from 1496. A. Thomas Skrine held a portion of the Warleigh estate as a copyholder under the monks of the Abbey at the time of its dissolution in 1536. The lands had remained in the Skrine family for four centuries. Educated at Hailebury public school, he attended Oxford University. Walter deVer Skrine enlisted in the British army and served as captain in the 78th Regiment. He came to Canada as a young man in 1883, settled near Calgary and purchased squatter's rights on land on Mosquito Creek in the High River area. He named his ranch the 'Bar S'.

Walter Skrine was an unsuccessful Northwest Territorial candidate for High River in 1898. Four years later he sold his ranch and returned to England. Later he was ordained to the priesthood and served as rector of Wooleigh, Devon. He died in 1943.

[See: Burke's Landed Gentry, 1972]

arthur leroy smith, k.c.

February 13, 1886 at Regina, Northwest Territories, son of Jacob Watson Smith and his wife Mary June Bole. He was of ethnic Scottish-Irish descent and an Anglican. Educated at Regina, he attended the University of Manitoba graduating in Arts. He then studied law and became a prominent Calgary lawyer. In 1921 he was an unsuccessful candidate for the Calgary East Federal riding.

Arthur Leroy Smith returned as the Progressive Conservative member for the Calgary West riding in 1945. He sat in the House of Commons for six years on the opposition side of the Chamber. In 1951 he vacated his seat due to illness and died the same year on December 17, 1951. (His son, Arthur Ryan Smith (q.v.) served in the Legislature from 1955 to 1957 and in the House of Commons from 1957 to 1963.)

[See: Canadian Who's Who, 1949]

arthur ryan smith, d.f.c.

Born May 16, 1919 at Calgary, son of Arthur Leroy Smith (q.v.) a lawyer and former Member of Parliament, and his wife Sara Ryan. He was of ethnic Scottish-Irish descent and an Anglican. He was educated at Shawinigan Lake School on Vancouver Island. At the outbreak of WWII, he enlisted in the Royal Air Force as an active service and as a Pathfinder pilot in Britain from 1939 to 1944. He was awarded the D.F.C. After the war he became a Calgary businessman and an executive in the petroleum industry. Active in civic politics, he served for two years as an alderman from 1953 to 1955.

Arthur Ryan Smith returned as a Progressive Conservative member for the multi-member Calgary constituency in 1955. He sat in the Legislature for two years when he vacated his seat to enter federal politics. He returned as the Progressive Conservative member for the Calgary South riding 1957 and sat in the House of Commons for six years. In 1963 he did not seek re-election and retired from politics at the age of 44. In 1998 he was still active in public life and a personal friend of Premier Ralph Klein. In October 1998 he retired from business at the age of 79.

[See: Canadian Who's Who , 1995]

s. bruce smith, q.c.

Born December 5, 1899 at Toronto, son of Frederick Howard Smith and his wife Kate Mark. He was of ethnic Scottish descent and an Anglican. He came to Alberta as a child, attended the University of Alberta, graduating in Arts in 1919 and then in Law in 1922. He was admitted to the Alberta Bar and became a prominent Edmonton lawyer in the legal firm of Smith Clement Parlee. He served on the city's Public School Board as a trustee.

S. Bruce Smith was named by Prime Minister Diefenbaker as Chairman of the Board of the Transport Commission in 1958. A year later he was appointed as a Justice of the Alberta Supreme Court: Trial Division. Following the death of Chief Justice Ford (q.v.) in February 1961, Justice S. Bruce Smith was appointed Chief Justice of Alberta and of the Court of Appeal, N.W.T. In 1974 he retired on reaching the age of 75.

[See: Canadian Who's Who, 1980]

barbara jane sparrow

Born July 11, 1935 at Toronto, daughter of Thomas Henry O'Connor and his wife Alice M. Rusgrove. She was of English/Irish descent and an Anglican. Educated at Havergal College, Toronto, she studied nursing at Wellesley Hospital School of Nursing. In recent years she has became a businesswoman in Calgary.

Barbara Jane Sparrow returned as the Progressive Conservative member for Calgary South in the general election of 1984. She sat in the House of Commons until 1993 serving the cabinet of Kim Campbell. She was re-elected in 1988 to the new riding of Calgary Southwest, but was defeated by Preston Manning in 1993.

[See: Canadian Parliamentary Guide, 1985]

william alexander stevenson, q.c.

Born May 7, 1934 at Edmonton. He was an Anglican. Educated at Edmonton, he attended the University of Alberta, graduating in Arts and then in Law in 1957. He articled with W.G. Morrow (latter Chief Justice Morrow of Alberta) and was admitted to the Alberta Bar in 1958. He practiced his profession in Edmonton with the legal firm of Morrow, Reynolds, and Stevenson. He was admitted to the Northwest Territories Bar in 1966 and the Yukon Bar in 1967. He also served as a professor in the Faculty of Law at the University of Alberta from 1968 to 1980.

William A. Stevenson was appointed as a Judge of the Northern Alberta District Court in 1975 by Justice Minister Otto Lang. When the courts were reorganized four years later, he was transferred to the Alberta Court of Queen's Bench and was elevated to the Alberta Appeal Court in 1980. On September 17, 1990 Justice W.A. Stevenson was named as a Justice of the Supreme Court of Canada, only the third Albertan to be named to that post. He vacated the Bench less than a year later because of poor health.

charles stewart (premier)

Born August 26, 1868 at Strathbane, Ontario, son of Charles Stewart and his wife Catherine. He was of Scottish descent and an Anglican. He came to Alberta where he homesteaded in the Killam District.

Charles Stewart first returned as Liberal member for the federal riding of Argenteuil, Quebec in the by-election of March 1922 and then from 1925 to 1935 as the Liberal member for the Edmonton West riding. In 1921 he was appointed as Minister for the Interior by Prime Minister Mackenzie King. He held the portfolio until 1930. In 1935 he was unsuccessful in his bid to be retired as the member for Jasper-Edson and retired from politics at the age of 67. He died in December 1946 at Ottawa.

[See: Canadian Who'Who, 1935]

charles stewart

Born March 26, 1917 at Edmonton, grandson of Charles Stewart (q.v.), one-time premier of Alberta and long-time federal cabinet minister. He was of Scottish descent and an Anglican. He was raised on the family farm near Hughenden. He became prominent Wainwright farmer and feed lot operator.

Charles Stewart returned as the Progressive Conservative member for Wainwright in 1979 and he sat in the Legislature for three years. In 1982, he did not seek re-election and retired from politics at the age of 65.

[See: Canadian Parliamentary Guide, 1981]

sir arthur allan **stonhouse**, 16th Baronet

Born February 24, 1885 at London, England, song of George Allan Stonhouse and his wife Ada, daughter of John Innes Allan. He was of English descent and an Anglican. His ancestor William Stonhouse of Badley, Berkshire created a baronet by King Charles II in 1628. Arthur Allan Stonhouse was educated at St. Paul's School, London and later qualified as a mining engineer. He came to Canada in 1905 and purchased land near Stettler, which he farmed for three years. He then moved to California where he worked as a mining engineer for eight years. Returning to Alberta to farm at Price Lake, near Red Deer, he became active in community and church affairs. At this time he built what is said to be the handsomest Anglican church in the province. He was an unsuccessful candidate for the provincial Legislature in 1935 and also unsuccessful in 1940 in a bid to enter the House of Commons. In 1937 Arthur A. Stonhouse succeeded his cousin in Sir Ernest Hay Stonhouse as the 16th Baronet. He died November 23, 1967 at Red Deer.

[See: Burke's Peerage and Baronage, 1978]

t

arthur williamson taylor

Born August 20, 1860 at Durham, England, son of Rev. James Jeremy Taylor, Anglican vicar of South Shields, and his wife Ester Oliver. He was of English descent and an Anglican .Educated at Durham Grammar School, he attended the University of Durham. He came to Canada in 1882, settled in Winnipeg and the federal Indian department where he worked closely with Edgar Dewney (q.v.). He worked for the government until 1892 when he went into real estate in Victoria, British Columbia. Later that decade he took part in the Klondike Gold Rush and became a wealthy man. He settled in Edmonton where Williamson Taylor was the president of the party in Edmonton in 1909. He unsuccessfully contested the Clearwater riding in 1913, but was defeated by Liberal H.W. McKenny. For many years he was one of the most prominent Conservatives in the province.

[See: History of Alberta, 1912]

f. fraser tims

Born February 8, 1856 at Berlin (now Kitchener), Ontario, son of Frank Dillon Tims and Caroline Dudley Fraser. On his paternal side he was of Anglo-Irish descent and an Anglican. He was educated at Ottawa and he attended the Quebec Commercial Academy. He came to the Northwest Territories as a young man where he became a commission agent.

F. Fraser Tims returned as the member for Victoria in 1894 and sat in the N.W.T. Legislature Assembly for four years. In 1898 he was defeated by J.W. Shera (q.v.) and retired from politics at the age of 42.

[See: Alberta: Past and Present, 1924]

frank austin walker

Born November 17, 1871 at Lucan, Ontario, son of William Walker and Catherina Spencer. He was an Anglican of Anglo-Irish descent. He came to western Canada as a child and was educated at Winnipeg and Edmonton. He became a prominent Fort Saskatchewan merchant and real estate agent. During WWI he served as an officer and went overseas with the Canadian Expeditionary Force. He saw active service on the Western Front.

Frank A. Walker returned to the first Alberta Legislature as the Liberal member for Victoria constituency. He sat in the chamber as government back bencher for 16 years. In 1921 he was defeated by the United Farmers of Alberta candidate, William Fedun. He then retired from politics at the age of 50. He died in 1956.

[See: Canadian Parliamentary Guide, 1921]

thomas john walker

Born October 20, 1927 at Armagh, Ulster, Northern Ireland, son of Thomas James Walker and his wife Florence Robinson. He was of Anglo-Irish descent and Anglican. Educated at Portumna, he attended Trinity College, Dublin graduating in Arts and then in Medicine in 1954. He emigrated to Canada in 1955, settling in Fort Macleod where he practiced his profession. He became a prominent physician in the area and established the Walker Clinic. From 1958 to 1964 he served as town councilor.

Dr. T. John Walker returned as the Progressive Conservative member for Macleod in 1975, and he sat in the Legislature for one term. In 1979 he did not seek re-election and retired from politics. He retired to British Columbia in 1993 and died June 6, 1998 at Victoria.

[See: Canadian Who's Who, 1979]

168 william leigh **walsh**, k.c.

Born January 28, 1857 at Simcoe, Upper Canada, son of Alquila Walsh, a member of Canada's first House of Commons, and his wife Jane Adams Wilson. He was of Anglo-Irish descent and of United Empire Loyalist stock, and an Anglican. Educated at Somcoe, he attended the University of Toronto. After being admitted to the Ontario Bar, he practiced law in Orangeville where he was a partner in the firm of Dalton L. McCarthy. He served three terms as the community mayor and was an unsuccessful candidate in the Ontario provincial election of 1896. In 1900 he moved to Dawson City, Yukon where he practiced law for four years. He finally moved to Calgary. He was an unsuccessful Alberta candidate in 1906. He served as the Chancellor of the Anglican Diocese of Calgary from 1929 to 1931.

William L. Walsh was appointed in 1912 as a Justice of the Alberta Supreme Court. Nine years later when the courts were reorganized, he was transferred to the Alberta Supreme Court: Trial Division. In 1931 he was elevated to the Appellate Division, but resigned from the Bench in May of that year on being appointed as Lieutenant Governor of Alberta. He held this position for five years. He died January 13, 1938 at Victoria British Columbia at the age of 81.

[See: Canadian Who's Who, 1936]

ernest shilston **watkins**, q.c.

Born June 18, 1902 at Liverpool, England, son of Richard Watkins and his wife Bessie Shilston. He was of ethnic English descent and an Anglican. He attended Liverpool University, graduating in Law in 1922. He practiced law in London from 1926 to 1939. During WWII he enlisted in the British Army and served in Iceland. He saw active service as a major in the artillery in Northwest Europe in 1944-1945. After the war he became a BBC commentator and assistant editor of The Economist (1945-54). In 1954 he wrote Prospect of Canada; coming to Canada in the same year, he settled at Calgary where he served as a crown prosecutor before setting up his law practice.

Ernest S. Watkins returned as the Progressive Conservative for Calgary in the October 2, 1957 city-wide by-election. He sat in the Legislature for six years as an opposition member. He was a candidate for the Alberta Progressive Conservative leadership in 1958 and again in 1962. In 1963 he retired from politics at the age of 60. He remained a Calgary lawyer and author. He wrote R.B. Bennett – Sketch in 1963 and Alberta: The Golden Province: Politics History, in 1980.

[See: Canadian Who's Who, 1970]

charles yardley **weaver**, d.s.o.

Born June 9, 1884 at Liverpool, England, son of Thomas Charles Weaver and his wife Laura. He was of English descent and an Anglican. He was educated at Manchester Grammar School. In 1903 he came to Western Canada as a Barr Colonist and homesteaded near Mannville. Later he attended the University of Alberta graduating in Law. He was admitted to the Alberta Bar in 1915. Previously he had enlisted in the First Edmonton Fusiliers in 1909. He became a sergeant two years later. He was commissioned a lieutenant in the Alberta Dragoons and two years later promoted to captain. He went to Europe as an officer with the 49th Battalion. He likely saw more front line active service then any other officer in the unit. He was awarded the Distinguished Service Order for bravery. By the autumn of 1918 he was second-in-command of the 49th Battalion in the last campaign of the war. After the war he became a prominent Edmonton lawyer. Active in civic politics, he served as an alderman from 1922 to 1923. Colonel Charles Y. Weaver returned as a Conservative member of the multi-member Edmonton constituency in 1926. He was re-elected in 1930, but died on October 1, 1930 at the age of 46.

[See: Canadian Parliamentary Guide, 1930]

william henry 'nobby' white

Born August 21, 1865 at City View, Canada West, son of John White and Sarah McAmmond. He was of English-Scottish descent and an Anglican. He was educated at Ottawa. He came to the Northwest Territories as a young man in 1881 to enlist in the Northwest Mounted Police. He served for six years with the Force and saw active service in the Northwest Rebellion in 1885. After resigning, he became a farmer-rancher near Fort Saskatchewan.

W.H. "Nobby' White returned as the Liberal member for Victoria (Alberta) riding in 1908. He sat in the Commons for 13 years. In the 1917 wartime federal election White was the only anti-conscription Laurier candidate to be elected in Alberta. The other 11 elected members were pro-Borden Unionist. At the time it was said that a large number of voters in the Victoria riding had been born in Scandinavia, or the German of Austrian empires and few spoke English. In 1921 White did not seek re-election and retired from politics at the age of 56. He died June 1930 at Fort Saskatchewan.

[See: Who's Who and Why, 1912]

frank edward wilkins

Born January 8, 1864 at the British Consulate in St. Louis, Missouri, United States, son of Francis Wilkins acting British vice-consul, and his American wife who was the daughter of George Steele, a prominent Chicago industrialist. He was of English descent and an Anglican. Educated at Edinburgh Academy, Scotland, he worked in Chicago. In 1884 his health failed and he travelled widely across North America. He decided to settle near Red Deer, Northwest Territories where he eventually became a prominent rancher and land developer.

Francis E. Wilkins returned as the member for Red Deer in the Northwest Territories Assembly in 1891. He sat in the Assembly for three years. In 1894 he was defeated by John A. Simpson and retired from politics. During the Klondike Gold Rush he managed the Yukon Navigation Company at Whitehorse. Later he returned to Red Deer and became the manager of the Blindman River Electrical Company. He committed suicide on May 13, 1908 at Lacombe.

[See: Men of Dwan, 1993]

w. roland winter

Born July 2, 1850 at Messina, Sicily, son of wealthy English parents. He was of English descent and an Anglican. Educated in England and France, he attended the Inns of Court, London and was admitted to the English Bar in 1872. He practiced law in England for 20 years. He came to Canada in 1893 and settled at Calgary where he first served as a magistrate. In 1900 he succeeded Horace Harvey (.v.) as registrar of the Southern Alberta Land Titles office and held the position for seven years.

W. Roland Winter was appointed by Justice Minister A.B. Aylesworth as judge of the Lethbridge District Court in 1907. Six years lather he transferred to the Calgary District Court. He vacated his seat on the Bench in 1926 and died February 23, 1929 at Calgary.

[See: Who's Who and Why, 1912]

henry woo

Born March 18, 1929 at Lethbridge, son of Ming Woo and his wife Idea Woo. He was of Chinese descent and an Anglican. Educated at Edmonton, he attended military courses at both naval and air force schools. From 1950 to 1955 he served in the Royal Canadian Air Force. He served on the federal cabinet sub-committee Indian Economic Development and was Executive Assistant to the federal Minister for Northern Development and Indian-Metis Laison. He was also Executive Assistant to the provincial Minsiter of Recreation, Parks, and Wildlife.

Henry Woo returned as the Progressive Conservative member for Sherwood Park in 1979 and he sat in the Legislature for 10 years. In 1989 he did not seek re-election and retired from politics at the age of 60. He was awarded the Order of Canada in December 1987.

[See: Edmonton Journal, March 1979]

eldon mattison **wooliams**, q.c.

Born April 12, 1916 at Roseton, Saskatchewan, son of Frank Wooliams and his wife Gertrude Mattison. He was of English descent and an Anglican. He attended the University of Saskatchewan, graduating in Arts and Law. He was called to the Bar of Saskatchewan in 1944 and of Alberta in 1952. He was an unsuccessful federal candidate in 1957.

Eldon Wooliams returned as Progressive Conservative member for Bow River riding in 1958 and he sat in the House of Commons for 25 years. He was the opposition justice critic in the 1970s but was not included in Joe Clark's cabinet following the 1979 election when the Progressive Conservatives formed the government. In 1980 he did not seek re-election and retired from politics, returning to his law practice in Calgary. He served on numerous international bodies during his politics career and maintained a very active involvement in a number of public service organizations throughout his life.

[See: Canadian Who's Who, 1958]

gordon samuel dales wright

Born June 28, 1927 at Kinston, Jamaica, son of Alwyn Dales Wright and his wife Mavis Parsons. He was of English descent and an Anglican. He was an unsuccessful candidate for the New Democratic Party in 1967, 1975, 1979 and 1982.

Gordon S. D. Wright returned as the New Democratic member for Edmonton Strathcona in 1986 and he sat in the Legislature for four years. He died October 18, 1990 while still an incumbent.

alfred wyndham

Born in 1937 in Blandford, Dorset, England, son of Captain Alexander Wyndham, who had served with Scotch Grey's regiment in the Battle of Waterloo. He was of English descent and an Anglican. Educated at the naval academy, he enlisted in the Wiltshire Militia as an ensign in 1855 and was sent to the Mediterranean on garrison duty at a number of posts there. In 1858 he left the Militia and came to Canada where he settled in Simcoe County. The next year he married Caroline Elizabeth Stuart, daughter of John Stuart, a prominent lawyer of Empire Loyalist stock. He became a prominent gentleman farmer in the area. While living in Simcoe, he maintained his connections with the military by joined the 12th Battalion – York Rangers. In 1882 he was appointed Lieutenant Colonel of the Militia Unit. At the outbreak of the 1885 Northwest Rebellion, Lt. Col. Wyndham commanded the York Rangers (militia) in the field. His regiment took part in the Battle at Batoche. After the revolt was crushed, he remained in the Northwest Territories, homesteading in the Carseland district east of Calgary. He became one of the most prominent early Alberta ranchers. Interested in Territorial politics, Col. Alfred Wyndham unsuccessfully contested High River constituency in 1898.

[See: Men of the Dawn, 1993]

www.ingramcontent.com/pod-product-compliance
Lightning Source LLC
Chambersburg PA
CBHW031553300426
44111CB00006BA/290